FOOD ADDICTION NO MORE

21 Days to Change Your Mind on Overeating for Good

MONIKA KLOECKNER

BALBOA.
PRESS

A DIVISION OF HAY HOUSE

Balboa Press books may be ordered through booksellers or by contacting:

Balboa Press
A Division of Hay House
1663 Liberty Drive
Bloomington, IN 47403
www.balboapress.com
1-(877) 407-4847

Because of the dynamic nature of the Internet, any web addresses or links contained in this book may have changed since publication and may no longer be valid. The views expressed in this work are solely those of the author and do not necessarily reflect the views of the publisher, and the publisher hereby disclaims any responsibility for them.

This book is not intended to prevent, diagnose, treat or cure any eating disorder. This book was written by a food addict who suffers from Polycystic Ovarian Syndrome (PCOS), not a physician or doctor. The author suffered from severe food cravings and emotional mood swings. The book describes a healing approach that is not approved by any qualified health professional or any statutory recognised medical health or medical professional body. The author wrote this book to share her personal approach to tackle her food cravings and emotional eating habits. The author has no training in medicine or nutritional therapy. **Please consult a licensed physician and nutritionist before beginning any new alternative or complementary therapy program.**

Neither the author nor the publishers of this book make any representations or warranties of any kind regarding the appropriateness of the advices contained herein for any individual. The information presented is not medical advice and is not given as medical advice, and is not a substitute for consultation with a specialist medical practitioner.

Any people depicted in stock imagery provided by Thinkstock are models, and such images are being used for illustrative purposes only.
Certain stock imagery © Thinkstock.

Printed in the United States of America.
ISBN: 978-1-4525-7878-1 (sc)
ISBN: 978-1-4525-7879-8 (e)

Library of Congress Control Number: 2013913582

Balboa Press rev. date: 8/27/2013

To The Creator of All That Is who pushed me gently from time to time to complete the book.

To Archangel Michael who reminded me that writing books is part of my life purpose.

To my mother who always knew that this book would be published one day.

To my soul mate Mark who rocks my world.

Table of Contents

Part I – Theta Healing™

Part II – Overcome your food addiction in 21 days

I. Well-being

VII. Inner Child Healing

VIII. Being at peace

Part III – Your chakras

Introduction

Have you ever thought that you can overcome your addiction to food by simply changing your negative beliefs in your subconscious mind?

I can assure you that this is possible.

Your subconscious mind holds beliefs, memories and experiences. They are stored like the information on a computer's hard drive and can be retrieved at any time again and again. You have hundreds of thousands beliefs stored in your human memory bank that can prevent you from overcoming your food addiction.

How is this possible?

The negative beliefs have been with you for a long time. Your beliefs can go back as far as seven generations. You have inherited beliefs from your ancestors. You hold beliefs and experiences from any past life you had before this one. All those beliefs your subconscious mind has accumulated are still held inside your mind. The more negative those beliefs are and the longer they have been with you the more they manifest in your body.

Your body mirrors the beliefs, thoughts and emotions inside your subconscious mind. If you don't like the body you see in the mirror than think about what you believe about yourself. How you see yourself and the world around you. Your body is the mirror of your beliefs.

Inside this book you will learn the most amazing belief change technique called theta healing.

In a nutshell, Theta Healing™ utilises the theta brain wave to tap into the subconscious mind where we find the answers to our unhelpful beliefs, thoughts and emotions. By asking open questions the beliefs hidden in the subconscious provide us with the answers to the issue. To test whether the belief is held on a subconscious level, the practitioner applies muscle testing. For those who have been treated by a kinesiology's, are familiar with the technique.

Inside this book I will be sharing 21 downloads that have been given to me by the Creator of All That Is in summer 2011. At the time the main focus in the media was weight gain and obesity. The discussion was why we have become so big over the century. Is it our lifestyle? Do we worry too much about our future? Or are most of us dealing with unsolved pain sustained in our childhood. Are we harbouring too many sorrows and grief in our heart? Whatever emotional or physical pain you are holding on to is going to be explored and unlocked in this book.

This book is written for my female readers who are dealing with long term food addiction. This can be emotional eating, binge eating or night time eating. If you feel that you have an unhealthy relationship to food then this book can help you overcome this addiction. However, this book is also suitable for male readers who struggle with food addiction.

I now invite you to join me on an amazing journey through the world of Theta Healing™ to begin healing your food addiction.

Food Addiction Test

Let's begin with a simple food addiction test.

This test determines whether you are a food addict. If you answer two or more questions with a YES, you can be sure that you are a food addict.

Do you overeat to numb your feelings of loneliness or depression?

Do you overeat because you don't feel good about yourself?

Do you overeat because you feel guilty for overeating?

Do you overeat because it gives you control over your emotions?

Do you overeat because you feel unloved by your parents?

Do you overeat because you reject your body?

Do you overeat because you feel disconnected from this world?

Do you overeat because you blame yourself for being abused as a child?

Do you overeat because you feel unloved by your partner?

Do you overeat because you don't feel the unconditional love of the Creator of All That Is?

By doing this test, you have found out whether you are a food addict. If you are dealing with unhealthy eating habits, you can now delve into the chapters and find out your deep seated beliefs and begin to heal on an emotional level.

The structure of the chapters

Part I—Theta Healing™

This first part deals in detail with the basics of theta healing, how to do belief change on all four levels, energy testing, how to connect to the Creator of All That Is and the feelings work. You learn what the key belief is and how you can find the key belief to change all other beliefs you may hold in your subconscious mind. You will discover that you are holding beliefs on four different levels. You are also going to learn step by step how to do self-healing to get your food addiction under control. At the end of part I you will find an example of a Theta Healing™ session.

Part II—21 days to overcome your food addiction

Each chapter begins with a download. This download represents the general idea if the chapter. I have written about my own experiences and thoughts on the subject in each of the chapters. At the end of each chapter you have the chance to do self-healing. You find exercises, digging suggestions, and questions to help you dig to the key belief and other useful information relevant to the subject. Day 4 includes a mirror exercise. In day 13 you will discover how to connect to the Creator of All That Is. Day 14 includes a love is all around you exercise. Day 17 shows you the soul fragment process and how to re-connect with your soul. In day 18 you are going to connect to your inner child through a meditation. Day 19 helps you to stay in contact with your inner child through various exercises.

How to use this book

This book is a tool to find out what kind of negative beliefs are held in your subconscious mind. For the purpose of finding out about these beliefs I suggest you buy or make a colourful notebook where you can record all your thoughts and insights. Make a note of whatever comes to mind about your life experiences beginning from childhood, how you think about your body and why you think like that. Explore your thoughts and beliefs about your mind, your inner child and whether you are at peace with yourself and the world.

You can use this book in the following ways:

1) You can read through the entire book from the beginning to the end; and you can work on your beliefs beginning with day 1 and complete your belief change work with day 21.

2) You can delve into the topic you would like to tackle first. It does not matter what day you would like to begin with and what day to finish with. I suggest that you follow your intuition on choosing the sequence of day to practise on.

3) Another option is that you pair up with a friend. Your friend does the energy testing, asks the questions and commands the Creator to do the changes. You can take turns on doing theta healing which is even more fund to do.

I suggest that you have a box of tissues beside you while you are conducting your own theta healing session. The deeper you dig the closer you get to the key belief, and that means the more emotional you become. Tears are natural, and releasing the emotions that have blocked you for years are part of the healing process.

My story

My food addiction began when I was in my early thirties. At the time my relationship with my boyfriend ended after almost five years being together. I had to live in a shared accommodation for a while again. I faced a few difficulties with various landladies. One was overpowering and watched my every step. She looked through my cupboards and tried to tell me what to eat. Being controlled was the last thing I needed. I moved out and rented a box room. It was a tiny room that made my soul shrink. The landlady in question and her husband loved to party. They organised a party almost every weekend. I felt as if I was confined to my box room because I was not invited to their parties. The music and the noise of the people made me crazy. And that is when I often met up with my friends and slept over at their place. This part of my life made me feel unsettled.

About six months later I was in the lucky position to buy my first own flat in London and I was the happiest person in the world. I moved into my flat and felt like a free person for the first time since I had left my parents' home in Germany.

I was also working with the airline I always wanted to work with. Unfortunately the work place was one hour drive each way from where I lived. The stress of getting up at dawn, driving down the M25 to Gatwick, dealing with the daily stress with passengers and long working hours took its toll on my eating habits.

I still was emotionally processing the end of my broken relationship. The purchase of the flat and the move were stressful. I now had to deal with unwelcomed work related stress too.

I just seemed to move from one stress situation to another. My mind, body and my soul didn't seem to agree with all the stress I created for myself. I started eating unhealthy food, such as Chinese take away, pizzas and crispy duck meals. I felt that I deserve to treat myself to something "tasty" once in a while. I spent almost every evening in front of the TV and consumed one unhealthy, fatty meal after another. When the stress was unbearable at work my colleagues and I would buy chocolate, coke and coffee. I began to eat one bar of chocolate at first. But soon I needed to satisfy my taste buds with at least two bars. The result was that my hips got bigger and bigger.

With the unsociable working hours and eating unhealthy food I always felt sad and depressed. Even when I was off work for one or two days I continued to eat comfort food. I couldn't be bothered to cook a healthy meal with fresh vegetables and lean meat. It was too much hassle to think about buying healthy food. That is why I always opted for the comfort food option. It goes in the microwave or oven and is ready to eat in minutes.

All my life I used to be slim. When I was a child I was stick thin. I always have been active riding my bike to school and friends, and attending table tennis classes. I also was a enthusiastic jazz dancer and was part of a jazz dance group in my home town. My mother always cooked healthy meals. She added herbs and spices. Her meals always were mouth watering. My parents also had strict eating times. At 7am we had breakfast together. Lunch was at 12pm and dinner at 7pm. The secret of being slim is to eat always at regular meal times. The second secret is that you eat in a friendly atmosphere were people talk to each other and make it a social event—every day.

Before I gained weight I was 60 kg light. I used to wear clothes size 12. When I started to gain weight uncontrollably I was about thirty two years old and had given up exercising and enjoyed my comfort food. Practically overnight I gained two pounds weight. And I continued to gain weight until I weighed 77 kg. I hated myself for the weight I accumulated. I didn't look at my body anymore. My clothes had become all too small. I felt sorry for myself. At the same time I hated the way I looked now. I had a fat face, fat arms, fat legs . . . and I could just go on like this. My clothes went from skinny to baggy.

I started to sign up for weight loss programmes and tried out numerous diet plans in magazines. The weight came off temporarily but it was not a permanent success. Soon after I stopped counting the calories of the foods I was supposed to eat I gained the weight again, and was often bigger than before. I was depressed, sad and fed up with my sad life. I had everything I always dreamed about: a lovely flat in London, my dream job with the airline I always wanted to work for and my untouchable freedom to do what I wanted to do. Unfortunately, because of the unsociable working hours the friends from the old times stayed away. I just couldn't get my emotions and my negative self-beliefs under control.

When I reached 77 kg I signed up with a weight loss clinic and they helped me to reduce my weight by 3 stones. After I lost 3 stones I felt younger, fitter and sexy. My skin glowed for health and my hair was shiny again. What a transformation I thought. I kept my weight off for more than four years. Honestly, I didn't pay attention to all the pizzas I was consuming again and the weight crept up.

Then in May 2010, I discovered theta healing at the Mind Body and Spirit Festival in London. I was attracted to the stands banner that said: Theta Healing™ changes your mind in an instant. Knowing that our mind and our body are connected, I wanted to know how theta healing works. I booked a taster session where the theta healing practitioner helped me to change my beliefs about relationship issues. After the session I felt unbelievably lighter and happier. I was convinced that theta healing would change my beliefs about me and the way I consume unhealthy food. I became a theta healing practitioner and have changed my body weight from 72 kg to 65 kg by just changing my beliefs and balancing my emotions with theta healing.

I have a medical condition called Polycystic Ovarian Syndrome (PCOS) which was only diagnosed when I was thirty seven years old. I had grown triple in size over a short period of time and was really unhappy about my weight and my looks. I was able to get my weight issue under control with a strict healthy diet. However, my emotional outbursts and food cravings still determined my life. My emotions and food cravings started to balance out when I studied Theta Healing™ and did belief change regularly.

Part I
Theta Healing™

Theta Healing™

Theta Healing™ was discovered and developed by Vianna Stibal, and American lady who once suffered from cancer in her right leg. She was told that she has a tumour in her right femur. Vianna was advised the only option would be to amputate the leg.

Vianna, an intuitive since childhood, studied Taoism and naturopathy. She gave intuitive readings to clients and soon noticed that she heard the Creator's voice.

One day, Vianna organized a family gathering. At the party her auntie had a bad stomach ache. To find out what could be wrong with her auntie she began to do a body scan. She then went out of the top of her head, through her crown chakra, and asked the Creator what is wrong with her auntie. Vianna was told that it was the giardia. She told it to go away and witnessed the Creator releasing the pain in her stomach. Within seconds, her pain had gone.

With exactly the same method, Vianna healed herself from cancer.

In theta healing sessions, the healing can take place instantly. But it also can take a week to heal or one month; or even a few months. It all depends on how many negative beliefs and thoughts are held in your subconscious mind.

You can read more about Vianna Stibal and her work on her website thetahealing.com.

Believers and Non-believers

Since I have become a theta healing practitioner I have promoted my healing business at numerous spiritual exhibitions and local fairs.

Whenever I talk to interested people at those fairs I meet a mixture of people who are totally curious about how Theta Healing™ works. Those are the people I love to work with. I do a taster session with them and they say "Wow", the healing works.

Then I come across sceptics. The sceptics have beliefs in their belief system that are holding them back to belief that the Creator of All That Is exists. They have learned that there is an energy source that has created this world, but because they have been disappointed in life, they have lost faith.

And then there are the cynics who come to my stand at the fair and they would say that theta healing does not work, because they think it is nonsense. I talked to one of those cynics at one of the local fairs. She told me that she has had back pain all her life and is on medication ever since. I invited her to try out theta healing just for about 10 minutes. I even said that if she is still sure that theta healing won't work I would return her £10 fee paid for the session. She agreed to it and I asked her about the back pain more questions. I then commanded the Creator of All That Is to let me know what the actual problem is. He subsequently showed me the lady living in another life. In that life she was handcuffed at the back and constantly beaten by her perpetrator. I told the lady what I had seen and asked her whether she would like to release the pain from the previous life. I also asked her whether she wants to forgive her perpetrator. The Creator released the pain. The lady felt already better when she left my stand. I advised her not to stop taking her prescribed medicine, but to watch her back pain. If it is getting better she can gradually stop taking the medicine. But she would need to consult her general practitioner first.

This lady was surprised that her back pain has its origin in a previous life. She didn't ask for the £ 10 to be reimbursed. I felt that I had convinced her with this taster session.

The belief in energy source, in Theta Healing™ we call it the Creator of All That Is, is essential if you embark on a self-healing session. Only then you will be able to witness your own healings. If you are a client you only need to believe in the healing.

You can be of any religion, and can call the Creator of All That Is the way you are used to it. This can be Shiva, Yahweh, Allah, God, or energy source, Jesus, Buddha or Jesus. All of those masters are connected to the 7th plane of Existence and the Creative Energy of All That Is.

Throughout this book I will be referring to energy source as the Creator of All That Is. But you can replace it with the name you are most comfortable with.

Your belief network

In Theta Healing™ sessions the practitioner helps the client to identify and change those stored beliefs known as programs.

We distinguish between four different belief levels.

1. Core level—these are the beliefs taught and accepted since childhood. Throughout our life we continue to learn new beliefs. Our beliefs are greatly influenced by our parents, teachers and the media. You find the core level beliefs at the frontal lobe of the brain.

2. Genetic level—these beliefs have been carried forward from your ancestors. We have inherited them and they have been added to our genes in this life time. The genetic level beliefs are found in the pineal gland, in the centre of the brain.

3. History level—these are beliefs and memories from previous life times or collective consciousness experiences. The history level beliefs are being changed behind the head and shoulders.

4. Soul level—you are the soul. This is essence of who you are. Grief, heartbreak and bereavement are held in the soul. The soul level beliefs are held at the heart chakra out to the aura field.

What is the key belief?

Imagine all the beliefs you have learnt and accepted in a form of a pyramid. The basis of the pyramid is the key belief that is holding all the other beliefs together. The key belief is the root of all the other beliefs above it.

Examples for key beliefs are: I am dead. I am nothing. I don't exist. I'll become nothing.

The goal in each healing session is to find the key belief because that is the one that holds the entire belief system together.

Important note: When you do self-healing on yourself, please note that you always need to use *positive wording*. For example you find out that you are not worth it. You need to energy test: I am worth it, no. Incorrect would be: I am not worth it. *The subconscious mind does not understand negative wordings.*

How do I know that I have reached the key belief?

You will know when you are getting close to the key belief when you

- Start to squirm
- Become emotional
- Start to feel uncomfortable
- Want to avoid the issue
- Wanting to leave the room

That is the point where you need to keep digging, because you are very close to find it.

The Four Commands

When you have found the key belief you go up out of your space to connect to the Creator of All That Is, and command the change of the limiting beliefs and to bring in the new belief. The word "command" is used in the prayer that is spoken to the Creator. For example:

"Creator of All That is, it is commanded that unconditional love is sent through every cell of this person's body. Thank you. It is done. It is done. It is done. Show me."

It is important to understand that you don't "tell" the Creator *of All That Is* to change a belief. You always need to use the word "command" in your prayers.

You can remember to use the word "command" as a signal to activate the change of your limiting beliefs and the healing in your body.

In the following exercise we are going to change the belief of "My body is beautiful". First, you need to energy test this belief. If you energy test with a "no", you need to do the belief change technique on all four level. And how it is done is explained here.

Take your journey to the 7th plane of existence.

The command to change beliefs on the core level (found at the frontal lobe in the brain) is as follows:

"Creator of All That Is, it is commanded that the core level programme of "My body is beautiful, no" held by myself be pulled, cancelled and sent to God's light, and replaced with "My body is beautiful". Thank you. It is done. It is done. Show me."

Take your awareness to your frontal love in the brain and witness the change of the belief.

Now you change the same belief "My body is beautiful, no" on the genetic level (found in the Pineal Gland):

"Creator of All That Is, it is commanded that the Genetic Level Programme of "My body is beautiful, no" held by myself be pulled, cancelled and sent to God's light, replaced with the programme God decides is for my highest good, for this to be done in the highest and best way. Thank you. It is done. It is done. It is done. Show me."

Take your awareness to your Pineal Gland and witness the change of the belief.

Now we do the same on the History level (found at the back of your head and your shoulders)

"Creator of All That Is, it is commanded that the History Level Programme of "My body is beautiful, no" held by myself be pulled, resolved and sent to God's light, replaced with the programme God decides is for my highest good, for this to be cone in the highest and best way. Thank you. It is done. It is done. It is done. Show me."

Take your awareness to the back of your neck and your shoulders and witness the change of the belief.

The fourth level where the theta healer changes beliefs is the soul level (found in the heart):

"Creator of All That Is, it is commanded that the Soul Level Programme of "My body is beautiful, no" held by myself be pulled, cancelled and sent to God's light, replaced with the programme God decides is for my highest good, for this to be done in the highest and best way. Thank you. It is done. It is done. It is done. Show me."

Take your awareness to your heart chakra and witness the belief change.

Take the journey to the 7th plane of existence.

To save time you can do all four belief changes simultaneously. And the command goes as follows:

"Creator of All That Is, it is commanded to remove the programme of "My body is beautiful, no" from myself on all four levels at one time, pulled, cancelled and replaced on all levels except the History level, which must be resolved and replaced, all replaced with the programme from the Creator that is for my highest good, in the highest and best way. Thank you. It is done. It is done. It is done. Show me."

Then visualize the healing/belief change taking place on all four levels, beginning with the genetic belief level, core level, history level and then soul level.

Please remember to witness the healing until it is completed. A healing that is not witnessed has not taken place. Please note that programs will recreate themselves if they are pulled on only one level, and not pulled on all four levels.

Explanation: THANK YOU—you express gratitude and the subconscious mind thinks the healing is done

IT IS DONE, IT IS DONE, IT IS DONE—this confirms that your subconscious mind that the healing has taken place

SHOW ME—this confirms to the Creator of All That Is that you are the witness to the healing

Feelings work

"I know what it feels like to live my daily life in happiness".

Not everybody knows what it feels like to be happy, to be joyful, to feel abundant. Feelings may have been forgotten when emotions of resentment, anger and hatred and unhelpful beliefs have taken over your life. Positive feelings can be re-learned. And that is what theta healing can help you with. During your self-healing session you work first on your beliefs, find the key belief, and have it healed by the Creator of All That is. Next, you instil the feelings have been given to you by the Creator of All That Is and instil them as follows:

1. Follow the meditation to the 7th plane of Existence
2. Make the command:

"Creator of All That Is, it is commanded to instil the feeling of (name the feeling) into myself through every cell of your body, on all four belief levels and in every area of my life, in the highest and best way. Thank you! It is done. It is done. It is done. Show me."

3. Visualize the energy of the feeling from the Creator flowing through every cell of your body and on all four belief levels, like a waterfall of white light.
4. Witness what you are shown by the Creator, until it is complete.
5. Ground yourself.

Following are some examples of feelings you may not have:

I understand what it feels like to be loved.

I know how to live my life without being stressed.

I know how to forgive myself.

I know how to live in peace with others.

I know how to live without being angry.

Energy testing

In theta healing sessions the practitioner applies the energy testing or muscle testing as it is applied in kinesiology. Muscle testing helps you to verify conscious and unconscious beliefs on all four levels. It verifies that a belief has been "pulled", and that a more helpful belief has come in.

You can choose to use the hand test or the standing test, whichever you are more comfortable with. The standing test is ideal for you if you suffer from arthritis or gout.

Hand test

Take the most dominant hand, and place the thumb and the middle finger together creating a circle. Then, take the thumb and middle finger of the other hand and use them as pliers whose job it is to test the strength of your dominant thumb/finger connection.

Let's try out the energy testing. To establish the pressure of your fingers please follow the instructions to form a circle with your fingers and say the following:

"My name is (say your name)". Then try to pull apart your fingers. These should not pull apart because your subconscious mind knows what your first name is. The answer is a yes.

Now say "I live in France". Then try to pull your fingers apart again. And this time you should be able to pull them apart. Your subconscious mind knows that you are not in France. The answer is a No. You can muscle test something else that is not true. However, if you are reading this book while living in France, you need to choose another country for this purpose.

Standing test

1. Stand upright and relax
2. Bend your knees a little and be in an impartial state.
3. Go forward to say YES, and as you do you will find that the weight of your body shifts to the front. It feels as if you are pulled forward.
4. Go backward to say NO, and as you do you will find that the weight of your body moves to the back.
5. Now try this out with a YES answer and a NO answer. My name is . . . and your body should pull forward slightly.
6. Now say: I live in London, and your body should move backwards if you do not live in London.

The 10 steps to successful self-healing

Step 1:
Before your self-healing session, drink plenty of water to hydrate your muscles. This is to ensure that your energy testing at the beginning and during the self-healing session works well. Only if your muscles are hydrated sufficiently you will get accurate yes and no answers to your questions. When you decide to do a self-healing session you may not have always water nearby. You then can hydrate your muscles by rubbing your kidneys. Alternatively, you can ask the Universe to hydrate your body.

Step 2:
Have the space cleared by the Creator of All That Is in the room where you do theta healing. The command goes as follows: "Creator of All That Is, it is commanded that my space is cleared now." Witness the clearing of the space. I always see spirits flying back to the light. With most theta healing sessions I have my deceased grandmother overseeing the healing session. Sometimes I have one of the Archangels standing by my side too. When the space is cleared the healings will flow easily.

Step 3:
Next, zip up your energy field. The main central energy flow is up the front body. When the flow is weakened the muscle testing may not work correctly. By zipping up your energy field you ensure that your energy testing works correctly. You zip up as follows: Imagine you zip your coat before going out. This needs to be done from the bottom to the top of your head, and from the left to the right side of your body.

Step 4:
At the beginning of each self-healing session begin by taking your consciousness to your heart, then ground yourself and connect to the Creator of All That

Is with the following command: *"Creator of All That Is, it is commanded by me to take away my conscious ego, so that I can hear, see and feel your divine guidance. Thank you. It is done. It is done. It is done. Show me."*

Step 5:
Energy testing can be done either with your hands or standing up. Please see chapter on energy testing.

Step 6:
Before you begin digging to the bottom belief I suggest that you open the seven main chakras. Chakras are energy centres running along our spine. The word chakra means "wheel" in the ancient Eastern language of Sanskrit. Chakras are known to push vital life energy through our body to ensure vitality. Effective healing can only take place when all chakras are open. Apply the following command to open your chakras. This will also open your psychic centres much more easily: *"Creator of All That is, it is commanded that my chakras be opened in the highest and best way. Thank you. It is done. It is done. It is done. Show me."* Beginning at the base chakra, visualise each chakra as it opens.

Step 7:
Dig to the key belief. Once you have found it you connect to the Creator of All That Is and command the changing of the negative beliefs and have them replaced with positive ones.

Although beliefs can be held only on one level, I always apply the command to have beliefs changed simultaneously.

The command is: *"Creator of All That Is, it is commanded to remove the programme (name the programme) from myself on all four levels at one time, pulled, cancelled and replaced on all levels except the History level, which must resolved and replaced, all replaced with the programme from Creator that is for my highest good, in the highest and best way. Thank you. It is done. It is done. It is done. Show me."*

Step 8: When you have had the beliefs changed into the positive you would like to teach yourself feelings. Please see chapter about feelings work.

Step 8:
Rinsing: Once you have finished your self-healing session you need to visualize rinsing off your consciousness to avoid leftover aches and pains of emotional baggage you may have picked up if you have done theta healing with a friend.

Step 9:
Grounding: After have completed your healing session you need to ground back into yourself. It is important that you once again send your energy-consciousness down into the centre of the earth, bring it back into your space.

Step 10:
Energy break: After you have grounded yourself you need to perform an energy break or so-called spiritual cleansing. You do the following: you visualize yourself rinsing off in white light or clear water as you enter back into your space with your consciousness.

Are you ready to receive healing?

I apply the following downloads at the beginning of a session with a client or when I do theta healing on myself. To begin a self-healing session with downloads about unconditional love and healing can help you safe time later in the session. Why? It is important to know whether you are ready to receive healing and whether you actually believe in healing. Your conscious mind might believe in healing, but your subconscious mind might not.

You need to do energy testing on the downloads below. If one or more of them are negative command the Creator of All That Is to teach you the download of unconditional love and healing.

Unconditional love

I understand the Creator's of All That Is definition of unconditional love.
My definition of unconditional love is the same.
I know how to receive unconditional love.
I am worthy of receiving unconditional love.
I deserve to receive unconditional love.
I am able to receive unconditional love now.

Healing

I understand the Creator's of All That Is definition of healing.
My definition is the same.
I know how to receive healing.
I know it is possible to receive healing.
I receive and accept healing now.

Visualization

Visualization is an integrate part of Theta Healing™. It is through visualization that we practitioners witness healings in our clients' body. We all have visualized at some point in our lives. You may have visualized yourself laying by a sunny beach, or having a rest on top of a mountain. We visualize daily, but we are not always aware of it.

Visualization for me is seeing pictures and moving pictures with my third eye. Often, I can hear the Creator's answers during healing sessions. And other times I just know that the healing has happened. When you visualize take you awareness to your third eye and practise "seeing" with it. What do you see when you imagine yourself laying by the beach (clairvoyance)? What do you hear (clairaudient)?

Choose one of the following visualizations and use your third eye.

1. Walk through your dream house or flat.
2. Your goal you have set yourself.
3. The country you would love to live in.

When you visualize one of the examples above, think about

- The colours you would see
- Who you would be with
- What you will hear
- How you would be feeling
- Who would you meet
- What you would learn

Visualization engages one or two of our psychic senses.

These are:

1. Clairvoyance (seeing)
2. Clairaudience (hearing)
3. Claircognizance (knowing)
4. Clairsentience (feeling)

These are the main psychic senses we experience in Theta Healing™. With practice you will find which one of these psychic are most developed within you.

The meditation to the 7th Plane of Existence

When you have established the key belief, you connect to the Creator of All That Is and command the healing of the limiting belief and the key belief. And you do this by applying the following meditation. I can assure you that you are not going to leave your room when you connect to the Creator of All That Is. You are safe and protected.

Begin with your awareness at your heart, taking that awareness to the centre of the earth and imagine there is a crystal at the centre of the earth that you connect to, then bring that grounding energy up through the bottom of your feet, up to the base of your spine. As you place your awareness on each chakra, observe it opening, spinning and clearing away any dust or debris that may be there. Begin with your base chakra, then your sacral, your solar plexus, your heart, your throat, your third eye and then your crown chakra at the top of your head.

Now take your awareness out of your crown chakra into a beautiful bubble of light, notice the colours and the sky, past the stars and the planets into the Universe. Now imagine going into the Light above the Universe. It is a big beautiful layer of bright white light. Imagine going through that Light, and you'll see another bright Light, and another, and another, in fact there are many bright Lights.

Keep going.

Between the layers of bright white Light there is a little layer of dark Light, but this is just a layer before the next bright Light. Then you will come to a layer of light jelly-white substance that has all the colours. In the distance, there is a pearly white iridescent light; it is a whit-blue colour, like a pearl. Head for that Light. You will see that the pearlescent light is the shape of a rectangle, like a window. This window is really the opening to the Seventh Plane. Now go through it. Go deep within it. See a deep, whitish glow go through your body.

Fee it go through your body. It feels light, but is has essence. It's as if you can no longer feel the separation between your own body and the energy. You become "All That Is".

While you are connected to the Creator of All that Is you then command the change of the beliefs you have found out and ask to be shown the new positive beliefs to be brought in.

Once the belief change is witnessed and completed you need to bring your awareness back to your body. Take you awareness down to the crystal at the centre of the earth. Then bring the grounded energy back up to your crown.

Our Chakras

Chakras are vortices through which energy flows both in and out the body. The word chakra comes from the Sanskrit, meaning "wheel" or "disk" and they are aligned along our spine from the root to the crown chakra at the top of our head.

Balanced chakras open up correctly and healings take place easily. If your chakras are too open it spins too fast or if the chakra is blocked it might not spin at all. You can take necessary action to balance those chakras by meditating on each chakra, or see a crystal healer who can help you balance your chakras again. Your chakras are also influenced by the food you eat. If you eat a lot of meat, especially red meat, drink coffee and alcohol, or eat sugary foods, your chakras won't spin correctly.

The chakras act like a series of valves in a system connecting a water tap to a garden hose. Once the tap is turned on, the water should flow smoothly through the system. But if there is a hitch in the system, the valves become blocked. This is comparable to a blockage of energy. If the valves are too open or too closed, this affects the proper functioning of the whole unit. That is why we need to open each of our chakras to an equal amount so that the "electrical current" of the Universal Life Force can be channelled into the body.

1st **chakra** is the root chakra, Muladhara in Sanskrit, is located at the base of your spine, between the anus and the genitals. Its colour is red. A balanced root chakra maintains equilibrium and spins at correct vibrational speed. It demonstrates self-mastery, high physical energy, is grounded and healthy.

2nd **chakra** is the sacral chakra, Svadhisthana in Sanskrit, is located at the lower abdomen, between the navel and the genitals. The sacral chakra's colour is orange. A person's balanced sacral chakra is trusting, attuned to her/his own feelings and is creative. But a person with an imbalanced chakra often deals with food addiction or any other addiction.

3rd chakra is the solar plexus, Manipura in Sanskrit, is located between the navel and the base of the sternum. This chakra's colour is yellow. A person with a balanced solar plexus respects herself and others, has personal power and is uninhibited.

4th chakra is the heart chakra, Anahata in Sanskrit, is located in the centre of the chest. Its colour is green. A person with a balanced heart chakra is compassionate, loves unconditionally, is nurturing, and desires spiritual experience in lovemaking.

5th chakra is the throat chakra, Vishuddha in Sanskrit, is located at the base of your neck. Its colour is blue. A person with a balanced throat chakra is a good communicator, is contented, finds it easy to meditate and is artistically inspired.

6th chakra is the Third Eye, Ajna in Sanskrit, is located above and in between the eyebrows. Its colour is indigo. A person with a balanced Third Eye chakra is charismatic, highly intuitive and is not attached to material things. In Theta Healing™ the third eye chakra is utilised for visualization and to witness healings.

7th chakra is the Crown chakra, Sahasrara in Sanskrit. The colours are violet, gold or white. A person with a balanced crown chakra has a magnetic personality, is at peace with herself and achieves "miracles" in life and is transcendent. When you send your consciousness through the crown chakra and connect to the Creator of All That is you are in theta.

The following command is going to open the psychic centres through the chakras. I command the opening of my chakras before each theta healing session with a client or at the beginning at a healing session with myself.

Here is how it works:

1. Centre yourself in your heart and visualize yourself going into Mother Earth, which is part of All That Is.
2. Visualize bringing up the Earth energy through your feet, opening up all your chakras as you go. Continue going up out of your crown chakra in a beautiful ball of light out to the universe.
3. Go beyond the universe, past the white lights, past the dark light, past the white light, past the jelly-like substance that is the Laws, into a pearly iridescent white light, into the Seventh Plane of Existence.
4. Make the command: "Creator of All That Is, it is commanded that my chakras be opened in the highest and best way. Thank you! It is done. It is done. It is done. Show me."

A Theta Healing™ session—example

Follow the steps explained in the chapter 10 steps to successful self-healing.

Please read the following digging session which I have conducted with my friend Maureen.

Healer: Let's begin this healing session with the download "I nourish my body only with healthy food."

I muscle tested Maureen on this download and the result is negative. This means I need to dig down on this download.

Healer: Why don't you know how to nourish your body only with healthy food?

Maureen: I am too lazy to cook.

H.: Why are you too lazy to cook?

M.: I have no time to think about cooking.

H.: What is happening in your life that you can't think of cooking?

M.: I am always busy.

H.: What do you mean by that?

M.: It is work, looking after my children, looking after my cats. There is always something that keeps me from cooking.

I muscle tested: I know how to prioritize my work. The answer was NO.

H.: Why don't you know how to prioritize?

M.: It has always been like that.

H.: Always?

M.: Yes, always. When I was a child I had problems tidying up. It was not my priority.

What happened in your childhood that you can't prioritize?

M.: My mother always tidied up my room while I was in kinder garden.

H.: What happened when you came home?

M.: I got angry when I saw that my mother invaded my space and tidied up. I ripped all the toys from the shelves and cupboards until it was untidy again.

H.: What happened then?

M.: What my mother saw the mess she got angry with me. She said that she tidied everything up and I would make a mess again.

H.: What is the worst thing that could happen when your mum is angry with you?

M.: She might resent me.

Muscle test: My mother resents me. The answer to this statement is NO.

Muscle test: I resent my mother. The answer to this statement is YES.

H.: Why do you resent your mother?

M.: She is controlling.

H.: How do you feel about that?

M.: I feel that I have no freedom.

H.: What is the worst thing about not having any freedom?

M.: I feel locked up.

H.: What is the worst thing to feel locked up?

M.: I can't get out.

H.: What is the worst thing about not getting out?

M.: I am trapped.

H.: What is the worst thing about being trapped?

M.: I feel like being dead.

Muscle test: I feel like being dead. The answer to this statement is NO.

Muscle test: I am dead. The answer to this statement is YES.

I am dead is the key belief to the download "I nourish my body only with healthy food."

Feelings work:

I know how to prioritize my work.

I know what it feels like to prioritize my work.

I know how to live my life without resentment.

I know how to live my life without conflict.

I understand what it feels like to live my life with freedom.

When you bring in the feelings you need to energy test them too. If you test negative you need to ask the Creator of All That Is to teach the feeling.

At the end of the session you integrate the healing, and say the following:

"Creator of All That Is, it is commanded that I am filled with unconditional love and that all the work I did be integrated now with grace and ease. It is done. It is done. It is done. Show me."

Part II
Overcome your
food addiction in 21 days

I. Well-being

Day 1: My self-esteem is growing day by day

Your self-esteem is greatly influenced by the experiences of your childhood. Experiences such as abuse, including emotional abuse or trauma are deeply stored in your subconscious mind. In the same way, the absence of emotional needs, such as affection, leave their imprints in your subconscious mind too.

However, if you had a happy childhood there is still a chance to develop low self-esteem in other areas of your life. These are divorce, bereavement of a loved one (person or pet), redundancy, bankruptcy or eviction from your own home.

I still remember how my self-esteem decreased. When I entered primary school I had a healthy self-esteem. I was bubbly, cheerful and was friends with everyone in my class. This changed when my maths teacher told me that I am useless at the subject. I would be able to learn foreign languages, but I would never learn the science of mathematics. That said, I took it to heart and believed what she said. She was the life experienced person after all. Being told at an early age that I am no good at mathematics influenced my decision not to apply for any job that would involve mathematics. In the end, I opted for a job in sales.

This scenario shows that children are influenced by adults at an early age. Most of us believe what we are told is true. With every unsatisfactory exam result in mathematics my self-esteem sunk more and more. I felt as if I have failed.

Here is another story which one of my best friends has told me.

Helga took private guitar lessons since she was eleven years old. In her group was just her and another girl. They both loved learning to play the instrument.

Helga's teacher seemed to have a crush on her. During one of the lessons he made a comment about her tight t-shirt. He thought that she looks like a real scout. He was breathing down her neck while he was showing her new accords on the guitar. Helga was not prepared for those unexpected advances. She confided in her parents. But they thought their daughter is making up excuses to cancel her guitar lessons. However, my friend stopped attending the classes in the end.

These two scenarios show that your low self-esteem has its roots in childhood. However, your self-esteem can crumble at any stage in your life.

Here are possible options:

- Divorce or relationship break-up
- Redundancy
- Failing your exams
- Bankruptcy
- Poor self-image
- Not feeling good enough
- Being humiliated in front of other people

Your self-esteem may have suffered in recent times, but I am sure that you have been able to succeed in several situations. You may not think that this is important to note, but it is. The more you think about the success you already had the more your self-esteem will rise again.

ΘΘΘΘ

Theta Healing™—Exercise

Digging suggestions:

I am good enough. I am loved. I am respected. I blame others (myself). I criticize others (myself).

Useful digging questions:

When did my self-esteem start to crumble?

How did I feel?

What happened?

When did it happen?

And then what would happen?

How do I know that?

What is the worst thing that could happen? (By asking this question repeatedly, you begin to dig deeper and deeper to the key core belief).

Keep asking open questions (How . . . ? When . . . ?, What . . . ?, Who . . . ?, Why . . . ?)

1. Using the 10 steps of successful self-healing
2. Connect with the Creator of All That Is by going up to the 7th plane of existence.
3. Allow the Creator to take your awareness to the relevant part of your brain.
4. Witness the healing until complete.
5. Ground yourself.

Day 2: I know how to live my life without stress

It may sound unusual, but my frustration about being overweight stresses me out. Does that apply to you too?

It stresses me out because I don't know why I can't overcome my food addiction. What I do know is that whenever I eat comfort food I feel pleasure at first. A short while later I feel guilty for eating thousands of calories again. Let us take a burger meal with fries and a soft drink. This meal has not only zero nutrition to offer, but feeds you with thousands of calories. They settle nicely on my hips. And that is where they stay for a very long time.

Guilt, frustration stresses me always out. I am frustrated because I don't know how I got so big in the first place. I don't know how to tackle the problem. I feel that there may be something wrong with me.

There must be something wrong with me because people in the street seem to stare at me because I am fat. The more often people stare at me I feel more and more rejected by society. I don't go out anymore. Whenever my friends ask me to join them on a night out I would find an excuse not to go. Most of my female friends were slim and I felt that I didn't fit in with the crowd I used to hang out anymore. I felt that they would judge me for being too fat.

When I got even more stressed due to work and commuting, I only found comfort in eating takeaway food and a bottle of wine. I enjoyed nights-in in front of the TV. This was my kind of relaxation after a hard day at work. I couldn't be more wrong.

I came to a point when I noticed that my hips had grown over my trousers. It was an ugly sight. I was not able to wear neither my size 12 jeans nor my skimpy T-shirts and blouses anymore. I had only two choices. First choice would be to accept that I have reached size 14 to 16, depending on the clothes I would try on. Or I had the choice to find out the reasons for my compulsive eating habit.

I started trying out various suggested diets in magazines. When the diets failed I joined a weight loss group. I learned from those diets that I have to restrict my calorie counting and I would reduce my weight. The thought of counting my calories stressed me out again. Other diets suggested that I have to omit eating certain foods. What? I thought I can't eat what I like? Stress set in again. Weight loss gurus all over the world suggest joining the gym to burn calories. When am I supposed to go to the gym? I work a forty hour week. All I can think of is stress. And that triggers my compulsive overeating habits.

What keeps your compulsive overeating going? What kind of stress triggers it?

ΘΘΘΘ

Theta Healing™—Exercise

Digging suggestions:

Success is mine. I know how to live my life without stress. I know how to relax. I am important. I identify stress and release it.

Useful digging questions:

When am I stressed?

Why I am stressed?

When was the first time I felt stressed?

How do I feel when I am stressed?

What stresses me out?

How do I know that?

What is the worst thing that could happen? (By asking this question repeatedly, you begin to dig deeper and deeper to the key core belief).

Keep asking open questions (How . . . ? When . . . ?, What . . . ?, Who . . . ?, Why . . . ?)

1. Using the 10 steps of successful self-healing
2. Connect with the Creator of All That Is by going up to the 7th plane of existence.
3. Allow the Creator to take your awareness to the relevant part of your brain.
4. Witness the healing until complete.
5. Ground yourself.

Day 3: I know how to implement exercise into your daily life

If you are like me, than you have already said too many times that you don't have time to exercise. I know exactly where you are coming from. I used to say that I have too much work to do. I work too many hours in the work. I need to relax when I am off work.

What does it look like when you relax? What do you do to relax? For me it meant that I would sit on my comfortable sofa and watch morning TV which that was extended into the afternoon. Watching TV can make you hungry. Researchers say that the more entertaining the program is the more you feel you need to eat. Whenever I watch a food commercial I can't help going into the kitchen to find something tasty. And that is usually not an apple or raw vegetables. My taste buds are demanding something like crisps or taco bells with a spicy dip. This is one of the reasons why I have gained weight so rapidly. No exercise, watching TV all day, and eating crisps and other high calorie foods.

Apart from not having the time I always was good at procrastinating. I always would say that I begin to exercise tomorrow. And straight away I came up with an excuse not to begin the next day because I would meet up with friends for a drink and dinner. Then I decided to start going for walks the next week. In the meantime I consumed pizzas, a bottle of wine and any other processed food I can imagine. When the next week arrived I was again not ready to start my exercises. I kept putting it off week by week.

The key to success is to take baby steps every day. First, determine what your long term goal is. Do you want to be physically fit? Or do you want to reduce your weight because you are getting married? As soon as you have established your goal you need to decide by when you want to have achieved it. In three months? In six months? In one year?

Promise yourself to start going for your first walk TODAY. Don't postpone it until tomorrow just because it is raining outside. It is fun going for a walk in the rain. Take your boots and your umbrella and off you go! Walk for just ten minutes and then walk back home. Increase your daily walk time by ten minutes. Burning off calories depends on how quick you walk.

A pedometer helped me to count the calories I lost. This pedometer also helped me to stay motivated. Because the more calories it showed me I had lost, the more I wanted to walk. Try it out if you like.

Naturally, you will experience set backs from time to time. These setbacks can be connected with work trouble, relationship issues, or with difficulties in paying your bills. Anything can throw you back into your sofa and you watch TV again, ruminating over the problems in your life.

When you experience any problems in your life your emotions come to the fore. Anger, frustration, anxiety, sadness, grief, or resentment plays an important part in overcoming procrastination. Any emotion or belief can get in the way of succeeding in engaging daily exercise.

The best way to find out what emotion or belief is keeping you from exercise is to find out what emotions it is that is holding you back. Find out when the problem not to be motivated started. Who is playing a significant role in your de-motivation? How did you feel when it happened? What would be the worst thing if you would never exercise again? What would be the long term implications?

Once you have found out what the key belief is in your situation you can move on. After releasing beliefs and replacing them with positive ones, you have gained new motivation.

You have achieved some success in regaining your motivation. How do you celebrate this little success? With every success I had in doing exercise I rewarded myself with a hot soaking bath and burned aromatherapy candles.

On other occasions I bought myself that book I wanted to read for a long time. Other options are treating me to a new manicure or massage, buying a new dress, or going to the cinema. It is needless to say that the reward should not be processed foods of any kind. You can work towards new rewards every week.

My own experience is that reducing your weight and getting fit does not happen overnight. It happens gradually. Begin with utmost determination and keep your goal in mind. I am sure you will succeed.

ΘΘΘΘ

Exercise:

1) Make a list of all the excuses you have not to do exercise.
2) Now make a list of how you can make time to implement exercise into your life TODAY!
3) What would you like to achieve with exercising? Do you want to exercise for health reasons? Or do you have other goals?
4) By what month do you want to have achieved the goal of exercising and reducing your weight?

ΘΘΘΘ

Theta Healing™—Exercise

Digging suggestions:

I know how to live my daily life doing exercise. I love exercise. I know how to implement exercise into my daily life. I like to exercise to relieve stress. I like to exercise.

Useful digging questions:

What is holding me back to start exercising regularly?

What would happen if . . . ?

What happened?

What happened next?

How do I know that?

What is the worst thing that could happen? (By asking this question repeatedly, you begin to dig deeper and deeper to the key core belief).

Keep asking open questions (How . . . ? When . . . ?, What . . . ?, Who . . . ?, Why . . . ?)

1. Apply the 10 steps of successful self-healing
2. Connect with the Creator of All That Is by going up to the 7th plane of existence.
3. Allow the Creator to take your awareness to the relevant part of your brain.
4. Witness the healing until complete.
5. Ground yourself

II. My body

Day 4: My body is beautiful

Whether you think your body is beautiful is influenced by quite a few factors. To me, the main factor of all is the mass media. Stick thin models on the cat walk and in magazines portray an incorrect image for teenagers and young people in their twenties. Girls as young as ten years of age go on diets for they want to look like their "role model" on the catwalk.

Unfortunately, even mannequins believe that being skinny equals confidence. But true confidence comes from the inside. If you accept yourself for the way you look, know your qualities as a human being, which means your personality and your intelligence, you will find it easier to find your body beautiful. Being beautiful does not mean that you can wear size 0. I once was very skinny. I reduced my weight by three stones and I looked very pale in my face. I had no curves left, but I thought that is what a woman needs to look like. My male colleagues acknowledged that I had the willpower to stay on a healthy diet for more than six months. But they also said that I don't look like a woman anymore, because I now have a flat chest and a flat bum. They asked me to gain some weight. So I did and I actually feel more feminine with my current curves. The picture of attractive skinny women has been impressed on us by the media. Real life men prefer "real" women with curves.

Please note that you have a beautiful body, no matter your dress size or visible scars you might have.

Many of you remember the British actress Dawn French. She is known for her role as a female vicar in the British series "The Vicar of Dibley" and various other roles in commercials and so on. She is a rather big lady, but she bursts with confidence, self-belief and humour. She is the proof that a woman doesn't need to be thin to be confident and have self-belief. Her laugh and happiness is irresistible.

Dawn French believes in herself, her values and qualities as a person.

The way you feel about your body image can be influenced by your parents' expectations. Their expectations and opinions about being slim also have been formed by their childhood experiences and the media. Unhelpful beliefs about looking slim and trim may give you the feeling not be loved and accepted as you are. It does not make you feel good. Being criticised by your own mother is never good. Our mothers often don't realize that their criticism can lead to low self-esteem, frustration and low moods. To make yourself feel better you eat comfort food. Reducing your weight may be a long way off. But we can't blame our mother for the well-meant suggestion to reduce our weight. She loves you and often she also believes in what the mass media tell us how to look. What I am saying is that our mothers want the best for us. They pick up other people's opinions from magazines, the news or the internet. They are as easily influenced by all the media frenzy as you are. The secret to success is to take one step at a time. A quick fix diet does not bring the results you are gaining for. Slowly does it, reducing your weight by one pound a week.

The puberty often sparks unhappiness about one's body image. This is a crucial time in your life. You might or might not be aware that the transition between childhood and adulthood is not easy. For most young women this time can be daunting and scary. And yet it can be exciting because you have entered the world of a grown up woman. Young men will acknowledge you for being feminine and attractive. It might not be your opinion about yourself. But people always see you differently than you see yourself. Be proud of your curves! Your body is beautiful the way it looks. Your curves are attractive. Celebrate them by buying yourself a flattering dress.

☻☻☻☻

Mirror exercise:

This is the "My body is beautiful—exercise": Stand in front of a full-length mirror or the largest you have. You can be dressed.

Advice: Your emotions will surface. Tears might come up. But this is all part of the healing process. I suggest that you have your notebook nearby and write down the emotions that will occur.

Begin by looking into the mirror and look at your body and face.

Then, say the following:

I love my eyes. They are bright blue and have dark long eyelashes.

I love my teeth. They are white and straight.

I like my legs. They are well-formed and sexy.

I like and accept my hands. They are small and feminine.

I love my smile. It makes me irresistible.

Every day for one week, stand in front of your mirror and say 5 nice things about your body and your face. They can be repetitive. The more beauty you see in your body and face the better. Continue to compliment yourself for your beautiful for as long as you wish.

Your subconscious mind registers this and after a while your mind has been changed into positive thinking about your body.

Body image issues can result from low self-esteem. Go back to Day 1 and dig on your self-esteem issues.

Day 5: I love my body more and more

How did the mirror exercise make you feel? Maybe it was difficult at first to look in the mirror and observe your body. Knowing that you need to look at your body in a mirror can make you feel uneasy, or even emotional. If it makes you feel emotional notice the thoughts and beliefs that come up. Make a note of them and dig on them until you find the key belief. Release and replace this key belief with a positive one. And then notice how you feel after the digging session. I can imagine you feel a lot better and happier.

But if you still not feel the love for your body maybe the following suggestions can help you to make a little progress.

Begin your body with kindness. How can you do that?

As you learned in the mirror exercise, have only kind thoughts about your body and your looks. Learning to love your body as it is takes time. It takes a good few months to fully accept your body. But the result will be well worth it.

Eat a healthy diet whenever you can. When purchasing fruit and vegetable make sure they are locally grown and are organic. Unlike foreign fruit and vegetables the local ones have not been treated with chemicals and pesticides. Ensure that you eat five fruit and vegetables a day.

Wear soft, natural clothes. Comfortable clothes made by nature's ingredients are a celebration for your skin. If you suffer from allergies with regards to chemically treated clothes you might want to swap those with natural ones. Wear clothes that flatter your body shape. If you are not sure about the clothes to wear, consult an image consultant. Image consultants can help you find your ideal colours and fabrics and will be able to give you advice how to dress best.

Book yourself a day at a spa and have a massage, manicure or pedicure. I sometimes book a whole day at the spa. Upon leaving I feel refreshed and energized.

If a day spa is too costly create your own spa at home. Make sure that you are alone at home so that you can't get distracted by any kind of noise. The idea is to totally relax and get back into touch with your senses and spirit. Whenever I hold a spa day at home I lit scented candles all over my bathroom and play spiritual music in the background. After you had the bath use baby oil to massage and re-hydrate your body. During your personal bath day only drink water and herbal teas. Eat a healthy stir fry and eat fruit. This will help you detox your body.

ΘΘΘΘ

Theta Healing™—Exercise

Digging suggestions:

I love my body. I accept my body. I cherish my body. The mirror is my friend. I feel good about myself.

Useful digging questions:

Why don't I love my body?

When did I resent my body for the first time?

What is the best thing that would happen if I love my body?

How would it make me feel?

What comes to mind?

How do I know that?

What is the worst thing that could happen? (By asking this question repeatedly, you begin to dig deeper and deeper to the key core belief).

Keep asking open questions (How . . . ? When . . . ?, What . . . ?, Who . . . ?, Why . . . ?)

1. Apply the 10 steps of successful self-healing
2. Connect with the Creator of All That Is by going up to the 7th plane of existence.
3. Allow the Creator to take your awareness to the relevant part of your brain.
4. Witness the healing until complete.
5. Ground yourself.

Day 6: I nourish my body only with healthy food

Surely, you know what healthy food is. There is no doubt about that. But do you nourish your body only with healthy food? I bet you can answer this question with a certain NO. So was mine. For most people it is the most difficult task to eat ONLY healthy food. From time to time even I need to eat something fatty or even comfort food.

I used to feel guilty whenever I ate chocolate or crisps. Deep down in my heart I knew that eating chocolate does not provide me with the necessary nutrition to keep my body healthy. But here and then I felt the urge to buy something unhealthy. And once I started eating one chocolate out of the package I ate the entire bar of chocolate. As soon as the moment of short lived happiness had faded I felt guilty for the treat I just enjoyed. I think you might experience the same kind of feelings.

You probably have tried to find out what the actual cause of your food cravings is. This might be easy to spot. Examples are boredom, feeling lonely, being stressed, being fed up with the way you life, fed up with work, not having a work/life balance and so on.

But there are beliefs attached to those food cravings and they are harder to find out because they are held in your subconscious mind. When doing a theta healing session on yourself, you will be finding out your deepest beliefs that trigger your food cravings. It can depend on memories from your childhood, your school life or an event that returns from time to time on your mind. Beliefs around these issues can trigger your food cravings.

Food cravings prevent you from eating only healthy food. You can have food cravings for sugary foods such as cake, donuts or chocolate. You might be addicted to caffeine, which includes coffee, tea and those energy drinks that are full of caffeine to make you feel more alert. Caffeine contains mercury. If you consume too much mercury your body will be depleted of its vitamins and minerals. Hence, your bones can become brittle. I have met people who are addicted to bread. Bread is baked with yeast, wheat flour and contains gluten. The same ingredients are found in pizza. I used to be addicted to pizza. Two years ago I ordered twenty three take away pizzas in only six months! I loved the taste of the pizzas, but my body felt bloated. My body weight increased slowly and steadily. My skin started to show signs of food allergies. I was diagnosed with dermatitis. Once you have developed a food allergy it is difficult to get rid of it. I tried healthy eating, followed my skin doctor's advice with temporary success. Eating healthy food alone is not the cure.

My other vice is drinking coffee. I used to drink up to five mugs of coffee per day. That was before I came across theta healing. Since I have been doing theta healing on myself, I only drink one or two cups of coffee per day.

By doing theta healing on my coffee addiction I found out that I harbour too much anger inside my soul. The belief "I am angry at the world" being the biggest belief I could find. Anything can be included in this kind of anger. You might be angry at the politicians, being angry at the way animals are treated, angry at the wealthy people who just seem to be too selfish to help the poor. With the word angry you can find out so much about your beliefs. It is amazing.

Food cravings can also be triggered by resentment. You might be resentful towards yourself or others. Here are many possibilities about resentment. Do the digging to explore. Ask yourself who do you resent and why. And then dig down to the key belief and command the Creator of All That Is to change it.

The more belief work you do the faster you will see results in eating more and more healthy food, much more often. The time will come and you eat only healthy food, and have lost the appetite to eat sugary foods, processed carbohydrates and caffeine.

ΘΘΘΘ

Theta Healing™—Exercise

Digging suggestions:

I nourish my body only with healthy food. I feel guilty. I am guilty. I resent others. I resent myself.

Useful digging questions:

What keeps me from nourishing my body only with healthy food?

How did I feel?

Who told you that?

How do I know that?

What is the worst thing that could happen? (By asking this question repeatedly, you begin to dig deeper and deeper to the key core belief).

Keep asking open questions (How . . . ? When . . . ?, What . . . ?, Who . . . ?, Why . . . ?)

1. Using the 10 steps of successful self-healing
2. Connect with the Creator of All That Is by going up to the 7th plane of existence.
3. Allow the Creator to take your awareness to the relevant part of your brain.
4. Witness the healing until complete.
5. Ground yourself.

Important advice!

You might have too much Candida in your body. Maybe this has happened due to taking antibiotics over a long period of time. Or you are addicted to sugary foods that might have caused Candida in your body.

In Theta Healing, avoid commanding all Candida to be gone from the body since many of the body's processes rely on some Candida to function.

Please also avoid removing all bacteria, heavy metals and vital minerals from your body. Your body needs some bacteria to live on. Your body is made up of many different kinds of heavy metals such as zinc and calcium. And without practice, the body does not understand how to assimilate minerals and vitamins in this way.

(Excerpt from: Disease and Disorder book by Vianna Stibal)

Day 7: I know how to nourish my body

Let's be honest. In general, you know how to nourish your body. You know how to distinguish between healthy and unhealthy food. You want to eat healthy nourishing food because it would make you feel and look healthy. You would have more energy and you would be less ill.

So, what is the problem?

I conversed with the Creator on this subject and he downloaded me the following message:

"Women would like to eat healthy food to nourish their bodies. They seem to think that their willpower is in the way. But this is only half the truth. It is not really the lack of willpower, it is the associated thoughts and emotions that make us feel weak. But they are not aware of it."

If your thoughts are similar to: "I really should eat healthy food, but I need to treat myself today because I had a stressful day at work." Your idea of treating yourself is to feed your body with toxins. Feeding your body with toxins, such as processed carbohydrates, pasta, take away meals and meals with chemical colourings is health damaging. I am sure you are aware of it. And yet, we all consume these foods on a regular basis.

If your thoughts are: "I really should eat healthy, but today I didn't feel loved. So, I need to get some Chinese take away and indulge the food."

You really are pushing down feelings of not being loved, of not being wanted or feeling lonely.

The Creator suggests that you learn to eat food to not only nourish your body, but to nourish your chakras. Eating food with natural colourings will give you plenty of energy and help you to stay healthy and fight off illness easy. But it also will help you to raise your vibration. Raising your vibration simply means that you radiate positive energy to the outer world. This shows itself in a glowing skin, clear and bright eyes, having lots of energy, and being able to cope with stress situations better.

You can raise your vibration by eating the foods that nourish the chakras. You will find a complete list of what foods to eat to keep your chakras healthy can be found in part III of this book.

ΘΘΘΘ

Theta Healing™—Exercise

Digging suggestions:

I know how to nourish my body. I enjoy the food I eat. I avoid fatty foods. My stomach is shrinking. I know how to nurture myself without overeating.

Useful digging questions:

What is the best thing that would happen if I would love my body?

What feelings are associated with this in which part of the body now?

How would I feel?

How do I know that?

What is the worst thing that could happen? (By asking this question repeatedly, you begin to dig deeper and deeper to the key core belief).

Keep asking open questions (How . . . ? When . . . ?, What . . . ?, Who . . . ?, Why . . . ?)

1. Using the 10 steps of successful self-healing
2. Connect with the Creator of All That Is by going up to the 7th plane of existence.
3. Allow the Creator to take your awareness to the relevant part of your brain.
4. Witness the healing until complete.
5. Ground yourself.

III. Relationships

Day 8: My partner loves me just as I am

You deserve to be loved just as you are. For some of us this seems to be a lifelong mission. It seems to be an enigma why your best friend is all loved up and lives a happy and content life with her partner, and you don't. If you are still single and have given up hope to find the man that would love and admire you, then please read on.

Your past relationship experiences shape your thinking and your future behaviour towards men. You approach potential lovers more cautiously. You may have lost trust and have become more critical about their advances.

Depending on how bad your relationships have been in the past, you may start sabotaging new relationships. I have been through this experience. When I met a nice guy, I thought he is probably too gorgeous for me and too intelligent. I formed negative thoughts about what he expects from a girl, how slim she has to be, and how intelligent she has to be. My thoughts about whether I would be able to live up to his expectations made me feel depressed. I didn't feel good enough and not worthy to be with him. I didn't have the confidence to admit that I am lovable jus as I am. It didn't occur to me that I have a lovely personality and intelligence and that I am a fun person to be with. Instead, I looked at my overweight figure and couldn't find anything attractive about myself. I was judging myself for my weight rather than for my personality. With my low self-esteem in mind I sabotaged every potential relationship that was about to blossom.

And when the beginning of this new relationship went wrong I said that I knew all along that he is not interested in me.

But what I have actually done is that my negative thinking has caused the disappointing result. Negative thinking is often accompanied by low self-esteem. The lower your self-esteem is the more negative thoughts you have in your mind.

Your negative thoughts and beliefs held in your subconscious mind show to the outside through your behaviour, your body language, your words, the sound of your voice.

Knowing that your partner loves you just as you are requires to do work from you. You need to explore your low self-esteem, self-sabotage and any negative thinking about yourself. It is the fear of being rejected that causes you to fail in having a loving and beneficial relationship. Clearing the fear of rejection helps you to live your life you desire and deserve. Love will flow to you in abundance. Men will respect you. They will do anything to be with you and to spoil you.

Here are a few points to consider when you have fallen in love with someone:

- Be sure to know that the man has fallen in love with you as a person.
- Be mysterious! Don't show off all your "assets" during the first date.
- You are worth to have a great guy in your life who treats you with respect from the first day he meets you.
- Don't fall for their criticism or judgement. A man who criticizes and judges you all the time is not happy with himself. Leave him to it and move on either alone or with someone else.
- There are guys out there who compare you with their previous girl-friend. I am sure you have experienced such a man before. They would say what a great cook she was and how well she always dresses. This is a sign that the man is not over his ex-girlfriend yet. This could make you feel less worth and less attractive. It is maybe a good idea to move on from this type of man too.

Where do you go from here? Ask yourself why you feel unloved when you are in a relationship. Find the key belief to the situation, release the negative beliefs and replace them positive and more helpful ones. I can assure you that you will attract the man who deserves you as soon as you have worked on your beliefs. This can take one month to work on or longer. I changed beliefs for almost a year when my lovely man came into my life. But it was worth the wait.

ΘΘΘΘ

Theta Healing™—Exercise

Digging suggestions:

My partner loves me just as I am. I am worthy of love. I sabotage my relationships. I love myself unconditionally. I can be loved by another person.

Useful digging questions:

What would happen if my partner didn't love me?

How would I feel about that?

When did I feel like this before?

How did I feel?

How do I know that?

What is the worst thing that could happen? (By asking this question repeatedly, you begin to dig deeper and deeper to the key belief).

Keep asking open questions (How . . . ? When . . . ?, What . . . ?, Who . . . ?, Why . . . ?)

1. Using the 10 steps of successful self-healing
2. Connect with the Creator of All That Is by going up to the 7th plane of existence.
3. Allow the Creator to take your awareness to the relevant part of your brain.
4. Witness the healing until complete.
5. Ground yourself.

Day 9: I am lovable

This chapter links in well with the previous chapter. The feeling of not being lovable can be depressing. I have felt like that in the past. There were times when I felt as if there is nothing lovable about me. I was criticised for being too fat, too shy and too sensitive. I was even criticised for being too cheerful. I felt that I can't get it right with anybody.

Whenever I felt unloved I would eat. I consumed take away meals almost on a daily basis. I couldn't get enough of the unhealthy food. I didn't notice that I was pushing down the frustration of not feeling loved by people, the sometimes never ending criticism and judgement I received. The more emotional I felt that more I ate.

A friend of mine once said that she loves me very much. You are a wonderful person to be friends with. You always have time to listen. You always help. Everything about you is lovable. The only problem you have is that you take criticism to heart.

Here I had it. I was lovable, but I took criticism too seriously. I conversed with the Creator of All That Is on this download, and he had the following message for me and you:

"I love you unconditionally, just the way you are. I think you are the most lovable person in the world. I love you with whatever you have done wrong in the past or present. I do not make differences between races, religions or gender. You are an amazing person, and you are absolutely lovable."

Energy source loves us the way we are. We are always connected with the Creator's energy. But we are not aware of it. As soon as we feel unloved, we feel deserted. We doubt whether there is a god. Many of us believe that if there is a god I would feel loved and accepted. I would receive help. I would not be left alone and deserted.

Since my friend told me that I am lovable, but take criticism too much to heart, I started to work on developing emotional resilience. It takes time to become a resilient person, but with persistence and willpower it can be achieved.

Here are my personal tips on how to become more resilient:

1. Build your self-esteem. Remind yourself of your strengths and accomplishments. Examine your beliefs on low self-esteem. Go back to day 1 and revise what you have discovered about yourself at the time.

2. I asked myself whether there is a different kind of work I could do, besides working in the corporate world. I started doing my research. The question I asked myself was: What kind of job would resonate with my personality? It is important that your personality matches the job you want to do. Only then you feel happy and fulfilled in your work. Let's say you are a caring person and have a natural ability to work with disabled children. That is the work where you belong with your heart and your soul.

   Doing research about my purpose, I found out that I wanted to serve people through coaching and healing. I signed up for a life coaching course which I immensely enjoyed studying. Every module kept me involved and I found joy in reaching my goal.

3. Think positive. I know that is not always easy, but it helps in the long run. When I started studying life coaching I visualised the positive outcome of working from home, coaching my clients to success. This visualization helped me to complete my coaching course with honours. Whatever you want to achieve in life, always visualize a positive outcome.

4. Establish goals in your life. Make a note of all the goals you have. Then prioritize what goals you would like to achieve within the next 3 months, 6 months and 1 year. Then focus on them I complete each goal at a time.

Remember, you are lovable for the way you are and that has been confirmed by the Creator of All That Is.

ΘΘΘΘ

Theta Healing™—Exercise

Digging suggestions:

I am lovable. I love myself. I love myself unconditionally. I am worthy of love. I understand the Universe's definition of pure love.

Useful digging questions:

Who says that I am not lovable?

Why did they say that?

When did I feel like this before?

How did I feel?

What is the worst thing that could happen? (By asking this question repeatedly, you begin to dig deeper and deeper to the key core belief).

Keep asking open questions (How . . . ? When . . . ?, What . . . ?, Who . . . ?, Why . . . ?)

1. Using the 10 steps of successful self-healing

2. Connect with the Creator of All That Is by going up to the 7th plane of existence.

3. Allow the Creator to take your awareness to the relevant part of your brain.

4. Witness the healing until complete.

5. Ground yourself.

IV. Your parents

Day 10: I am loved by my father

In conquering the underlying issues of your food addiction you need to examine your relationship to your father.

Your food addiction might have been triggered by a traumatic event in your childhood. You know what it might be that triggered off your unhealthy eating habits. This might be emotional abuse, physical abuse, mental abuse or sexual abuse.

Any kind of abuse can turn into feeling resentment towards to abuser. The longer the resentment stays within your mind it eventually manifests around your body. If resentments are not dealt with at all they can turn into anger and then into hatred. Any of these emotions are of low vibration, but with digging and getting to the core of the issue it can be healed.

At some point in our lives we cannot make our father responsible for his abusive behaviour anymore. We need to take responsibility for our childhood experiences. This may sound tough, but it also means that we have taken on the role of a victim. While we were victims of abuse at the time, it does not help us to move forward in life if we stay in the role of a victim. When we grow older we owe it to us to let go of the negativity that has accompanied us since our childhood. Now is time to let go of any hurt and pain. The time has come to forgive and accept the past. It can't be changed but we can make peace with it.

Remember that your father once might have been the victim of abuse. He might not have felt the love he was craving. He probably felt being alone. Maybe he didn't feel wanted. Fathers usually don't talk about their feelings. They are very good in hiding them. They have learned not to cry in front of others because it makes them look like a girl. Instead your father kept his feelings buried and never let them out. Abuse is one way of letting out anger from the past.

However, I believe that father and daughter can be friends. Both need to leave behind their difficult years and can move on. The father needs to recognise that mistakes have been made, and that those mistakes have shaped the daughter's view on men. It has influenced your thinking about your men. It might be mainly negative due to the fact that your father has not treated you with love and respect. Not knowing any differently, you attract unconsciously men who would not treat you with respect.

I remember that a friend of mine, let's call her Betty, had an abusive father. He abused her emotionally. On several occasions, she had to go to bed without having dinner because she was too bubbly and cheerful.

The signal Betty received was the following:

- When I misbehave I have to go to bed without food. It is meant to be her dad's punishment for disturbing his quiet dinner.

More than often Betty's father used to say that she has to eat up her plate. Only then the sun would shine.

- This puts pressure on Betty to eat everything she has on the plate, although she was full up already. If we are forced to stuff down our food as a child we always will feel forced to eat up everything that is on our plate. The result is that we overeat later in life and gain weight we can't shed off anymore. A great amount of emotions are responsible for this unhealthy eating habit.

Sometimes she had to sit on a chair in the corner because she walked through the entrance hall with dirty shoes. My friend felt humiliated because she didn't know what she had done wrong. She was punished in one way or another whenever the occasion arose.

- When your father humiliates you and punishes you in some way, you feel unloved. You feel as if something might be wrong with you. You think that you are very bad so that your father needs to be angry with you and reprimand you in some way. Feeling unloved during childhood can lead to food addiction later in life. The feelings of shame and guilt have manifested in your subconscious mind. They also might show on your hips and waist. Emotions that are not being dealt with manifest in your body.

Whatever experiences you have endured during your childhood, now is the time to let go of hatred, anger, or resentment. Only if you release and replace those negative feelings towards your family you will be able to move on with your life. Your relationship with your father may become better too.

ΘΘΘΘ

Theta Healing™—Exercise

Digging suggestions:

I am loved by my father. I resent my father. I hate my father. I am angry at my father. My father loves me.

Useful digging questions:

When did my father abuse/humiliate me for the first time?

When did I feel like this before?

What happened?

When did I resent my father for the first time?

What happened then?

What is the worst thing that could happen? (By asking this question repeatedly, you begin to dig deeper and deeper to the key core belief).

Keep asking open questions (How . . . ? When . . . ?, What . . . ?, Who . . . ?, Why . . . ?)

1. Using the 10 steps of successful self-healing
2. Connect with the Creator of All That Is by going up to the 7th plane of existence.
3. Allow the Creator to take your awareness to the relevant part of your brain.
4. Witness the healing until complete.
5. Ground yourself.

Hatred and Forgiveness

Release the hate, cancel it and send it to God's light to be replaced with "I release" or "I forgive":

"I understand what it feels like to forgive my father".

"I am good enough to be forgiven".

"I know what it feels like to forgive myself".

Once you have released the hatred, you also have to set free programmes such as "I am angry with my father" or "I resent my father".

Day 11: I am loved by my mother

Every daughter is loved by her mother in her own way. The way your mother shows her love to you depends on how she has experienced her mother's love in her childhood.

Our mother loves us with all her heart. Sometimes we don't seem to think like that at all. There are times when she criticises us for being too big, for the hairdo she doesn't like, for our dress sense, for the food we eat and so on. I think that this list is not exhaustive. Although our mother does mean it well and is not aware of her over-critical behaviour, we often think that she is just out to hurt us. Well, I can say with confidence that most of the mothers don't even realize that they criticise us constantly. They see their criticism as help offering. Their mother instinct is still fully functioning when you have already moved out and have your own family or live your own life. To her you always will be her baby. It is nice to know that your mother still cares that deeply when you are already an adult, but it can make you feel controlled.

Unfortunately, mothers seem to have the tendency to control their daughters. Control issues in any case can originate from jealousy. I have experienced mothers who are jealous of their daughter's independent way of life, their freedom to choose what they want to do with their lives. The need to control their daughter can also mean that the mother is insecure and just can't let go. She simply does not understand that the daughter is an adult and makes her own decisions. It can be hard for a mother to understand that the daughter needs to make her own decision and has to learn from her own mistakes. This is part of life.

Despite the control issues and the criticism I truly believe that our mothers love us the way we are. We need to understand that our mother has maybe experienced a difficult childhood or her life is not progressing the way she hoped for. She needs a bit of understanding in this case. Nevertheless, being criticised or being controlled is not the way forward in a mother and daughter relationship. If you are a sensitive person you might become secretive. You might take your mother's criticism to heart and as a result you might lose confidence. Talk to your mother about her criticism. She surely might say that she didn't mean to hurt you. And a chat with your mother can clear the air between you and her.

ΘΘΘΘ

Theta Healing™—Exercise

Free yourself from your mother's obligation to criticise you by asking the following questions:

How is my mother's criticism serving me?

Is my mother's criticism motivating me?

Does she constantly tell me I can't do something?

Is my mother's criticism keeping me from moving forward?

Is your mother's criticism making you upset or depressed? Free her from this obligation.

And here is how it works:

Energy test: I know how to exist without conflict. If it tests negative you need to pull the programme of "This person motivates me by conflict". Then replace this programme with "I free this person from the obligation of creating conflict in my life".

Digging suggestions:

I am loved by my mother. My mother loves me. My mother criticises. My mother respects me. My mother accepts me for the way I am.

Useful digging questions:

Why don't I feel loved by your mother?

Why do I feel offended by my mother's criticism?

Why am I offended by her criticism?

When did I feel like this before?

How did I feel?

What is the worst thing that could happen? (By asking this question repeatedly, you begin to dig deeper and deeper to the key core belief).

Keep asking open questions (How . . . ? When . . . ?, What . . . ?, Who . . . ?, Why . . . ?)

1. Using the 10 steps of successful self-healing
2. Connect with the Creator of All That Is by going up to the 7th plane of existence.
3. Allow the Creator to take your awareness to the relevant part of your brain.
4. Witness the healing until complete.
5. Ground yourself.

Day 12: I know how to live my life without rejection

Every one of us has been rejected for one or the other reason.

You felt rejected by your partner for breaking up with you. Was it really your fault? You may have come to the conclusion that your partner had the issues. He still had to deal with problems from a previous relationship. He may be dealing with anxiety of the future. There are so many options to think of.

You applied for a well-paid job and didn't get the position. You feel rejected. This may not be directed at you personally. There are often unknown reasons for not getting job. But think about it. When one door closes another one opens up. I am sure, that there is a better job waiting for you.

I certainly was in the position a few times. For many years I always felt rejected. Before a relationship begun I feared to be rejected. So I sabotaged it right from the start. I did the same when I applied for a job. I instantly assumed that I would not get it. I felt rejected at work. I felt rejected all the time.

Then I got to the bottom of the issue, and changed my negative thinking into the positive.

Negative thinking would be: I feel like such a failure. I knew I would not get the job. I knew he would break up with me sooner or later. Everything is my fault. You feel hurt. You blame yourself for the failure you experience. With every rejection you experience your self-esteem lowers more and more.

So, how can you overcome your rejection?

Every rejection can help you learn from it and move forward with success. Ask yourself what went wrong? Why did it happen? How can I improve? As a matter of fact, you grow from each rejection you experience. It might hurt at the time and you might feel that this is unfair. But bottom line is that you grow and learn from it, and you will be stronger afterwards.

Find out why you always feel rejected. Think back to your childhood. Is there someone who rejected you? The solution to the issue often goes back childhood years.

ΘΘΘΘ

Theta Healing™—Exercise

Digging suggestions:

I feel rejected. I am rejected. I am a failure. I feel like a failure.

Useful digging questions:

When did I feel rejected for the first time?

When did I feel like this before?

How did I feel?

What happened?

How do I know that?

What is the worst thing that could happen? (By asking this question repeatedly, you begin to dig deeper and deeper to the key core belief).

Keep asking open questions (How . . . ? When . . . ?, What . . . ?, Who . . . ?, Why . . . ?)

1. Using the 10 steps of successful self-healing

2. Connect with the Creator of All That Is by going up to the 7th plane of existence.

3. Allow the Creator to take your awareness to the relevant part of your brain.

4. Witness the healing until complete.

5. Ground yourself.

Instil the feeling "I know how to live my life with rejection".

V. Unconditional Love

Day 13: You are loved unconditionally by the Creator of All That Is

Unconditional love is a love that makes you feel safe. You feel understood. You feel wanted and accepted. You feel connected with people and with yourself. You are listened to whenever you express your opinion. You are never judged or punished for your actions. You are loved unconditionally whatever you do wrong or right in your life.

Sounds wonderful, doesn't it?

Like a loving parent, you are loved unconditionally by the Creator of All That Is. The Creator's unconditionally love makes you feel like living on a white beautiful cloud day in and day out.

You might have experienced moments in your life when you were convinced that there might not be a God. To question the existence of a God is a normal reaction to the negative experiences you endure in our lives. These experiences can be rooted in our childhood. When children's essential needs, such as hugs and kisses are missing in their lives, children do not feel loved. In some cases children think that there might be no God, because they feel alone or lonely.

Let me tell you my own story. There was a time in my life when I thought that God does not exist or would punish me. I was made redundant from my first job after I left school. It was a well paid job with great career prospects. I was not properly trained for the duties I had. Whenever I asked for help I did not get the help I needed to exceed in my job. This resulted in making mistakes that could have been prevented if I had received appropriate training. However, I was made redundant. My world fell apart and I got angry at God. I blamed God for leaving me alone in this situation and started to doubt that a God exists.

Temporarily, I lost my faith in God. I took a step back from my catholic faith. Prior to my redundancy, other things in my life had gone wrong as well. But my faith in God restored quickly when I found a new job quickly after my redundancy.

There is a reason why we go through bad times in life. The reason is that you create your live with your thoughts. For example, you are invited to a job interview. You have been told that there are twenty other competitors for the same position. What is your first thought? Your first thought might be that you won't get the job because there are other interviewees. You give up before you get to the interview. With your negative thoughts in mind, you take part in the interview. Your negative thoughts vibrate from your aura, the energy field around your body. A person with good personal skills senses the negativity and low self-esteem that surrounds you. A company is more likely to employ someone who demonstrates positivity during the interview.

The more negative thoughts you hold in your subconscious mind the more you attract negative situations into your life.

Whenever you are going through a rough patch in life you might have attracted this situation with your negative thinking. Whatever thought you send into the universe, the universe will give you exactly what you think.

There are times in your life when you feel unloved and not protected. The following meditation helps you to feel loved by being wrapped up in a bubble of white light from the inside out. The White Light is the unconditional love of the Creator of All That Is.

ΘΘΘΘ

Theta Healing™—Exercise

Connect to the Creator of All That Is

1. Sit down somewhere quiet and relax. Breathe in and breathe out. Breathe in and breathe out. Breathe in and breathe out. Let go of all your thoughts until your mind is still.
2. Begin beneath your feet and draw energy from the centre of the Earth.
3. Draw this energy up into yourself.
4. This automatically opens the chakras and activates kundalini instantaneously.
5. With the energy of kundalini, the connection is made with the Creator of All That Is of the Seventh Plane of Existence

After you have done this exercise you will feel connected to the Creator of All That Is. You can repeat this exercise if you feel you need to.

Kundalini is the energy that lies dormant at the base of the spine until it is activated and channelled upward through the chakras in the process of spiritual perfection. (thefreedirectory.com)

Day 14: I know that love is all around me

I know that love is all around me. Often though, I do not see that it is. Then I was shown to open my eyes, my mind and my heart. I noticed that love can be found in the most unlikely places.

When I see someone help an old lady cross the road, I see love.

When a stranger opens the door for me, I see and feel love.

When the cashier at the till offers me to pack my shopping bags, I see and experience love.

When a friend listens to me, I see and feel love.

When I see the trees and flowers blossoming in the park and in my garden, I see the unconditional love of our Creator.

When my cat twinkles at me, I see and feel her love.

When a colleague offers her or his help with a task, I see and feel love.

Have you come across love today?

Love is well and truly all around you. You only have to recognize it.

ΘΘΘΘ

Love is all around me—exercise

Please do the following:

Walk through your town and look for situations and moments where you can see and feel love. You will be amazed what you will discover.

Think about other situations where your family, friends and strangers have shown their love towards you.

Remind yourself every day that love is around you, even if you live in a city that is build in concrete. You will see and find the love there too.

Day 15: I know how to live my life receiving love

In the last chapter we have established that love is all around us, but we only have to see and recognize this love. Receiving love is synonymous for accepting and receiving help or any other act of kindness.

Sometimes the love is subtle, but sometimes we are not aware of the love others show us. Sometimes we just don't see the love. We believe it is too good to be true to receive love.

Those are the moments of doubt. We think that we are not good enough to receive honest love from others. There are people out there who give love without expecting anything in return. Those are the people who love unconditionally. They accept you with your looks and your personality. They would help you at any time. Those are the people who radiate love from their inside out. They always would go above and beyond to be there for you. It is safe to accept their help at any time.

But have you ever experienced the kind of love that is conditional? With conditional love is meant that someone puts a condition on the help they offer you. For example, I used to have a colleague who usually helped in order to ask for a favour in return. Once she offered me to work for me on her day off, so that I could off work the day I needed. I had a dentist appointment that day and was not able to get the time off. At first it looked as a complete act of kindness and I thought that her thought to work for me on her day off is lovely. I was grateful and thanked her. However, a few weeks later she reminded me of her favour and asked for a favour in return. She was planning to go shopping with a friend in London. And she picked one of my days off to do that. I gave in and did her the favour.

There are other signs of receiving conditional love. Parents often say to their children things like: "If you are a good girl today I treat you to your favourite McDonald's meal".

"If you tidy up your room I buy your favourite biscuits".

When you behave well or do things exceptionally well for your parents they treat you to unhealthy food. They also put a condition on the subject and that is a sure path into becoming a food addict later in life.

These experiences from your childhood are deeply ingrained into your subconscious mind. So when you do well at work or think you deserve a treat, you eat an unhealthy take away meal or indulge into chocolates and biscuits. While eating the comfort food you push down feelings of frustration, of feeling alone, of not being loved. You didn't receive love the way you should have experienced it.

However, there is always a chance that you can change those feelings. As adults we need to take responsibility for our life. Whatever has happened to us up until now in your life can't be undone. The beliefs about love or the absence of love has shaped your thinking and your life.

Beliefs, we have discovered can be changed. We only have to find the key belief.

ΘΘΘΘ

Healing™—Exercise

Digging suggestions:

I am worthy of love. I know how to live my life receiving love. I am good enough to receive love. It is safe to receive love.

Useful digging questions:

When did I experience unconditional love for the first time?

What was it like?

When did I feel like this before?

How did I feel?

What happened? What happened next?

What is the worst thing that could happen? (By asking this question repeatedly, you begin to dig deeper and deeper to the key core belief).

Keep asking open questions (How . . . ? When . . . ?, What . . . ?, Who . . . ?, Why . . . ?)

1. Using the 10 steps of successful self-healing
2. Connect with the Creator of All That Is by going up to the 7th plane of existence.
3. Allow the Creator to take your awareness to the relevant part of your brain.
4. Witness the healing until complete.
5. Ground yourself.

Day 16: I know how to live my life giving love

Giving love without asking anything in return is rewarding and brings of sense of being connected to other people. The following affirmations are meant to give you an idea what giving love means.

Affirmations:

Giving love makes me happy and content

Giving love connects me to the Creator of All That Is

Giving love opens my heart to attract love

Giving love involves kindness, gentleness and patience

Giving love raises my vibration

Giving love to self means self-acceptance and worthiness

Giving love connects me to my Inner Child

Giving love gives me a sense of being at peace with myself

This list is by no means exhaustive. Please feel free to write your own affirmation list on giving love.

Giving love is not easy when you have not experienced receiving love as a child. The way we receive love is exactly the way we give love. A child that has been abused does not know what it is like to give love. Love is absent in their lives. How can they know what giving love does mean. They need to learn slowly to develop the act of giving love in small steps.

Giving love can be learned. The process of giving love can take time. First, it is important to know that love is around you. There is always one kind person you speak to during the day. Help often comes out of nowhere. Those people show you that they give love. It is a matter of becoming aware of the love that is given to you.

Take note of other people's kindness and begin to do the same.

I once attended a seminar where I learned how to build my spiritual business. One of the speakers in particular stood out. He explained that he writes a complimentary note to every person who treats him well. He mentioned the example of a shop assistant who went above and beyond for him to find a particular article in the store. He in turn wrote a note of gratitude to the manager. The sales assistant was overwhelmed with joy. For every gratitude note you send out you will receive the same gratitude back. The more gratitude you practise the more abundance comes into your life.

For me, practising gratitude is giving love. The person who receives the gratitude note feels loved, accepted and honoured.

Giving love creates a cycle of eternal love. You give love, you make people happy. The people you give love to return the love by showing you their love. Wouldn't it be a wonderful world if all would give love on a regular basis?

Here are 5 ways to show your love:

1.   Donate your unwanted gifts, clothes, china and bags to charity. There is always someone out there who would be happy to have what you don't like anymore. This act of kindness is called de-cluttering your home and de-cluttering your life. You free up blocked energy in your property or room. This has the advantage that abundance flows into your life. This can be new friends, money, health and well-being.

2. Work as a volunteer in a charity shop or at a charity centre. Choose the charity of your choice and commit yourself to helping there once a week.

3. You can show love by simply listening to your friend's problems. Leave behind your work or hobby for an hour and listen what your friend has to say. It might be just a matter of being there for her or him. Sometimes a friend just needs to let go of the "mess" that is going on in their lives. They feel better when a trusted friend listens.

4. Treat a friend who has been there for you with a nice meal. This would be a meal you cook at home. Find out what your friend's favourite meal is and prepare for her.

5. Another act of love is to send someone a "thank you" card for their help. This is a simple but effective way of saying "I love you".

Obviously, you can only give love freely if you have forgiven those who didn't treat you with love. Those are often people who are close to you (family, friends, school mates and colleagues). Whatever negative experiences you have learned throughout your life you need to forgive them. Resentment, anger and holding grudges can block you to give love.

Why is it important to forgive? Forgiveness will help you to give love, but also to receive love. You would experience higher energy levels, and you can focus on your projects better.

ΘΘΘΘ

Theta Healing™—Exercise 1

Find out what emotions you are holding in your heart. You can find out best by doing the following exercise:

• Centre yourself and let go of any negative thoughts in your head
• Take your awareness to your heart

- Visualise your heart—Is it dark red? Does it have many emotions to deal with?
- Ask your heart what emotions it is aware of.
- Sit still and wait for an answer. It may take a minute or so until you get an answer. It all depends how still your mind can be.
- As soon as you receive the answer, connect with the Creator of All That Is and command the healing of all the emotions and replace them with love and forgiveness.

ΘΘΘΘ

Theta Healing™—Exercise 2

Digging suggestions:

I know how to live my life giving love. I know how to live my life forgiving others. I know how to forgive myself.

Useful digging questions:

Who do I want to forgive?

When did I feel like this before?

How did I feel?

What happened?

How do I know that?

What is the worst thing that could happen? (By asking this question repeatedly, you begin to dig deeper and deeper to the key core belief).

Keep asking open questions (How . . . ? When . . . ?, What . . . ?, Who . . . ?, Why . . . ?)

1. Using the 10 steps of successful self-healing
2. Connect with the Creator of All That Is by going up to the 7th plane of existence.
3. Allow the Creator to take your awareness to the relevant part of your brain.
4. Witness the healing until complete.
5. Ground yourself.

VI. Soul Healing

Day 17: I am disconnected from my soul

Your soul is the immortal essence of you. It is the emotional centre through you live. Without your soul your body can't exist.

How can the soul get disconnected from the body? Your soul disconnects itself from your body when you have been abused as a child. This can be emotional abuse, physical, and sexual abuse. You suppress the emotional feelings of your abuse, but you still feel the pain and the hurt. You have become used to it, but you don't know how to heal the past.

Whenever you remember the past, it feels as if you relive the abuse all over again. You feel angry towards the abuser. You resent what happened to you when you were most vulnerable. No one was able to help you because you were ashamed of what happened to you. You blamed yourself and you felt guilty.

When you suffer, your soul suffers too. Your soul is your essence and your body lives through your soul. All the decisions you make are directed by your soul.

You know when you are disconnected from your soul you overeat or become an alcoholic.

There are other reasons why your soul could be disconnected.

When someone you loved with all your heart breaks up with you, you leave a part of your soul with that person.

When you have lost a loved one through bereavement or in an accident, than one part of your soul stays with that person. This can even apply to a soul mate you have been together with in a previous life.

Another option of your soul feeling disconnected would be a location you have visited and still have fond memories of. If this is the only happiness you have experienced than your soul would stay with that location you loved so much.

How can you reconnect with your soul? Please go to exercise 1.

ΘΘΘΘ

Exercise 1:

In this exercise I ask you to get in touch with your soul. Write a letter to your soul. Have pen and paper ready or make a note in your notebook. This exercise was given to me by the Creator of All That Is.

1. Sit down somewhere quiet and relax. Close your eyes and let go of all negative thoughts you might have.
2. Centre yourself by breathing in and out three times. To be able to relax better you can listen to meditation music.
3. Once you are relaxed and feel the peace inside you, imagine inside you a white blue coloured spinning disc. This is your soul.
4. Your soul is the essence of you and therefore harbours all your feelings, emotions and beliefs. Ask your soul whether it is happy. How can I nurture you to make you happy? What can I do to re-connect with you?
5. Make a note of every answer you get from your soul. And begin to make the necessary changes in your life.

ΘΘΘΘ

Theta Healing™—Exercise 2:

1. Centre yourself in your heart and visualize going down into Mother Earth, which is a part of All That Is.

2. Visualize bringing up energy through your feet, opening each chakra to the crown chakra. In a beautiful ball of light, go out of the universe.

3. Go beyond the universe, past the white lights, past the dark light, past the white light, past the jelly-white substance that is the Laws, into a pearly iridescent white light, into the Seventh Plane of Existence.

4. Make the command:

5. "Creator of All That Is, it is commanded that all soul fragments from all generations of time, eternity and between times from me be released from them, cleansed and returned to me. It is commanded that all soul fragments belonging to (name of the person) be released from myself, cleansed and returned to them as is proper for this time. Thank you! It is done. It is done. It is done. Show me."

6. Witness the fragments as they are returned.

7. As soon as the process is finished, rinse yourself off and put yourself back into your space. Go into the Earth, pull Earth energy up through all your chakras to your crown chakra and make an energy break.

VII. Inner Child Healing

Day 18: My inner child is loved

Your inner child is the part of your personality that still reacts like a child. Your inner child can be male or female. It is about three or four years old.

My inner child is three and a half years old. His name is Thomas. Thomas is blond with blue eyes and has a lovely smile. He wears a multi-coloured shirt, jeans and trainers. He looks very mature for his age.

How do I know what my inner child's name is and what he looks like? I connected to him. You can connect to your inner child with the meditation in the exercise at the end of this chapter.

Thomas has experienced trauma at the age of two and a half years. He burned himself with hot water. Thomas fought for his life in hospital for three months. The doctors didn't give him much chance of survival. But against the odds, Thomas survived. He is a fighter.

If you have experienced trauma, abuse or neglect in your life how do you feel? You are hurt, you are angry, you feel lonely and sad. You might be scared and have lost trust in the people who were supposed to love and safeguard you. You become quiet and feel disconnected from life and society, because you have no one to turn to for support. And that is exactly how your inner child feels. Your inner child feels like you and he or she feels with you.

When I burnt myself, my mother experienced trauma as well. Years after the event she told me that she relives the moment I burnt myself over and over again. She has never really overcome the trauma of her young daughter being burnt by hot water. She felts guilty of not being fast enough to stop the inevitable to happen. Whenever she saw my scars on my chest she felt the pain I experienced when I pulled the boiling water towards my little body. Her pain was healed during my basic theta healing course in May 2010. During a theta healing demonstration session in front of the class my inner child was healed and the trauma of the burns sustained healed me and my family. In theta healing sessions we can heal pain, trauma and beliefs seven generations back. This means that also my grandparents who were there at the time have had healed their pain about the trauma.

ΘΘΘΘ

Try this meditation to connect with your inner child.

1. Begin by noticing what you are feeling and when you are feeling it.
2. Take some time to breathe and relax into the feelings.
3. Imagine that there is a little girl or boy inside you having these feelings.

This child is the young, underdeveloped part of you. You may have an image or just a gut sense or inner knowing.

4. Ask yourself these questions: "How old is this child? What is this child's name? What kind of attention does this child want from me right now? Does he or she feel loved?

The child may want to be reassured or held, or he or she may just want to know that he or she is loved.

5. If possible, imagine giving the child what he or she wants.
6. Continue to commune with this child for as long as you like, giving and receiving words or physical contact, as appropriate.
7. When you are done, notice how you feel.

You may be relaxed or confident—or at least less upset or afraid.

8. Be sure to give your inner child a hug (if the child feels comfortable receiving one), tell the child that you love him or her, and reassure the child that you will check in with him or her again from time to time.

When your inner child feels loved then you feel loved too.

Day 19: My inner child wants to play

When was the last time you played like a child? Can't remember? When I was a child I played every day. My parents had a large garden and I had all the garden toys to play with. I had a see saw, a swing, a kid's swimming pool in summer and a sand box which was most fun. I invited my friends into our home and we would play together for hours.

Even as adults we need to keep alive the inner child inside us. This inner child wants to play because he or she never grows up. When we play around foolishly with kids toys and behave like children once in a while we often feel guilty. On several occasions I heard myself saying: Now that was childish. I hope no one has seen me behaving like a child on that see saw. There is no need to feel guilty. When you feel like running around like a happy child, then just let it out, your "inner child". This inner child wants to play from time to time. Loosen up and let go of the adult behaviour and don't think about our people's opinions. Your inner child wants to play and wants to get excited again.

How do you get more excitement back into your life?

Here is an idea: Organise a pyjama party where you tell your friends to wear childlike pyjamas. Play with them the game bobbing apples and get totally excited over it. If you haven't played musical chairs or Pin the tail on the donkey, now is the time to play children's games again.

If you prefer to be more creative on your own try out a painting class or a creative writing course. When you don't know what to play ask your inner child, and he or she will tell you. If you are not sure how to connect to your inner child, follow the exercise from day 18.

I used to collect souvenir dolls on my travels. I would place them into a special shelf at home. When I collected so many dolls that they couldn't fit into my shelf anymore I started to collect silver spoons. If you have never collected anything ask your inner child what he or she wants to collect. Go into a toy store and buy your inner child a present. This may be a small teddy or a doll, depending on your inner child's gender.

However, not everybody knows how to revive the inner child in themselves. Due to childhood abuse, trauma or rape you might have never experienced carefree days. In those cases your inner child has gone deep into hiding. It is scared to play and to be happy. In this case you need to teach your inner child how to play. Be patient with yourself and make daily baby steps. When you start to eat comfort food ask your inner child whether it really needs to eat the food. How is your inner child feeling? Ask your inner child whether he or she is physically or emotionally hungry. Maybe it is just to suppress emotions? Find out what your inner child really wants.

ΘΘΘΘ

Exercise:

I suggest you take notes on what your inner child "tells" you. This helps you to analyze your true emotions and why you overeat. Analyzing your emotions will help with any digging work you would like to do. Take note of any beliefs that come up and dig down to the key belief.

Stay in contact with your inner child on a regular basis. Write a letter to your inner child. Your inner child would feel loved and respected. He knows that he is not forgotten. Staying in touch with your inner child also means that you grow your intuition. Your inner child is also known as your intuition. We often ignore our intuition when we are in a dangerous situation. Our intuition tells us to stay out of the situation, but we often ignore feelings like that. By staying in contact with your inner child you will become consciously aware of any unpleasant situations and can react accordingly.

VIII. Being at peace

Day 20: I know how to be at peace with myself

As you have learned throughout this book, food addiction can be caused by numerous factors: abuse in childhood or later in life, unhappy relationships, low self-esteem and feeling unloved. Upsetting thoughts about people who insulted you, abused you and have upset you in any way have made you feel angry. Every time those thoughts come up in your mind you get upset again and again. The result of this is that you don't feel the peace inside you.

You can feel resentment towards people who treated you unfairly, judged and criticised you. You can't change the other person, but you can let go of the anger and resentment that has build up in your body, mind and your soul.

Reasons for not being at peace are:

1) Being angry at other people for being disadvantaged in some way because of your weight, looks or nationality,
2) Being criticised by others constantly,
3) Complaining about the weather, the late trains, the bus that never arrives, the messy daughter, the messy son, the ever increasing utility bills . . . the complaining just does not stop. It takes away so much energy, it is unbelievable.
4) Worries about what other people think about you, their opinions about your looks, want you wear and what you say also takes away your energy. You might find that worrying makes you tired, because it leaves you with no energy left in your body.
5) Self-doubt. When you doubt that you can't achieve your goal, whatever that goal might be, the nagging thoughts that you might have failed will be with you all your life.

Any of those reasons create negative thoughts that can stay with you for many years. They manifest in your mind, body and soul. They become programmes that are anchored deeply in your psyche. But as you know, it all can be changed into the positive.

When you have worked on your beliefs you will easily recognise that you are at peace when

1) People can't upset you anymore,
2) You feel less stressed,
3) You radiate calmness and love,
4) You are happy; happiness always shines from the inside out,
5) You are able to focus what is important in your life,
6) You experience effortlessness, flow, and harmony
7) You experience the joy in everything you do and every person you meet.

Living a life in peace is possible. Achieving peace takes time. But by noticing your negative thoughts and actions a first step towards inner peace is made. The moment you don't get upset about other people's criticism anymore you have achieved inner peace. When you found inner peace you stop overeating.

ΘΘΘΘ

Theta Healing™—Exercise

Digging suggestions:

I am at peace with myself. I am at peace with the world. I know how to live my life with peace in my heart. I know how to forgive myself.

Useful digging questions:

When do I feel not being at peace?

When did I feel like this before?

How did I feel?

What happened?

How do I know that?

What is the worst thing that could happen? (By asking this question repeatedly, you begin to dig deeper and deeper to the key core belief).

Keep asking open questions (How . . . ? When . . . ?, What . . . ?, Who . . . ?, Why . . . ?)

1. Using the 10 steps of successful self-healing
2. Connect with the Creator of All That Is by going up to the 7th plane of existence.
3. Allow the Creator to take your awareness to the relevant part of your brain.
4. Witness the healing until complete.
5. Ground yourself

Instil the following feelings LOVE, HAPPINESS, JOY

I know how to live my life giving love.

I already know how to live my life giving love.

I understand what it feels like to receive love.

I understand what it feels like to be happy.

I understand what it feels like to have joy.

But also instil the feeling of "I know how to live my life without being angry".

And: "I understand how to forgive myself". "I understand how to forgive others".

Day 21: I know how to be at peace with others

As much as you want to be accepted and loved for the person you are, so do the people you meet too. The art of being at peace with others is that you do not criticise them or judge being at peace with others is that you meet them with an open mind. Keep a positive outlook at all times.

When you are at inner peace with others you radiate it to the outside. Friends and family will notice a change in you. They will at first not being able to pinpoint what has changed in you, but they noticed your openness, your friendly disposition and that you are talking to them in a non-judgemental way. Mind you, that you vibrate your thoughts and opinions to the outside world through your aura. Let's have a look at this from your point of view. Let's assume that you are at a party. Most of the other guests have already arrived. You sit somewhere where you have a good view of the room and the guests. Suddenly the last guest arrives. This guest gives off a vibration of calm and happiness. Just by looking at her you would know instantly that she is a nice person to talk to and that you are able to trust her. A person who is at peace with others naturally loves everybody unconditionally. Vice versa, a person who is not at peace with others vibrates bitterness, unhappiness and makes other people unhappy with their actions and behaviour.

The more inner peace you practice the more inner peace you vibrate to the outside and towards others.

ΘΘΘΘ

Theta Healing™—Exercise

Digging suggestions:

I am at peace with others. I vibrate serenity. People love me. I love people. I love everyone unconditionally.

Useful digging questions:

Why am I not at peace with others?

What makes you angry?

When did I feel like this before?

How did I feel?

How do I know that?

What is the worst thing that could happen? (By asking this question repeatedly, you begin to dig deeper and deeper to the key core belief).

Keep asking open questions (How . . . ? When . . . ?, What . . . ?, Who . . . ?, Why . . . ?)

1. Using the 10 steps of successful self-healing
2. Connect with the Creator of All That Is by going up to the 7th plane of existence.
3. Allow the Creator to take your awareness to the relevant part of your brain.
4. Witness the healing until complete.
5. Ground yourself

Part III
Your chakras

Nourishment for your chakras

You have already learned that our chakras are our energy centres. They are situated inside along our spine inside our body. When only one of these chakras is out of balance your health can be out of balance and theta healing does not work well either. Apart from opening the chakras all in the same way is one important step. But you also need to nourish your chakras to keep yourself healthy and to get clear answers from the Creator of All That Is.

Your chakras can be closed if you drink too much caffeine or alcohol. Try also to refrain from eating too much red meat or white bread. Eat as much organic fruit and vegetables as possible.

Here is a list of what each chakra need to be nourished with to keep the healthy balance in your body.

Root—, or Base Chakra—Sex, Money, Power

Eat red foods to

- Have a healthy appetite,
- Have a healthy sex-drive,
- Control and stimulate the kidneys and bladder,
- Nourish the muscular system

Foods to eat: strawberries, red cherries, red plums, damsons, water melon, rhubarb, raspberries, red currants, red apples, red lentils, red kidney beans, black-eyed beans, aduki beans, beetroot, radishes, red peppers, tomatoes, red chillies, Spinach, mustard and cress, red and black sea vegetables, red-skinned potatoes, red onions, black pepper, mustard cayenne, peppermint, mint, rosemary, rooibos tea, cranberry juice.

Sacral Chakra—Inner Child issues

Eat orange foods to

- Activate the sexual organs,
- Boost your self-confidence and self-respect
- Build up your immune system
- Promote the absorption of calcium

<u>Foods to eat</u>: oranges, mangoes, peaches, apricots, nectarines, papaya, orange lentils, carrots, Swedes, orange, melons, pawpaw, mango, whole pumpkin, butternut squash, brown skinned onions, turnips, ginger, paprika, cumin, coriander, mace, nutmeg, saffron, cardamom, apple cider vinegar, egg yolk, white cheeses, dark honey.

Solar Plexus chakra—Survival Issues

Eat yellow foods to

- Strengthen your nervous system and muscles, including the heart creating a better circulation,
- Alkalize your body,
- Increase concentration,
- Promote open-mindedness and communication of thoughts.

<u>Foods to eat</u>: wild rice, wheat, buckwheat, millet, bulghar wheat, cornmeal, rye, barley, oats, mung dahl, chickpeas, all nuts and seeds, golden apples, hazel pear, apricots, bananas, pineapples, corn, yellow peppers, yams, parsnips, gem squash, pumpkin, white radish, marrow, caraway, cumin, turmeric, cinnamon, nutmeg, butter, unsaturated vegetable oils, corn oil, light honey.

Heart Chakra—healing of emotional hurts

Eat green foods to

- Balance stress,
- Have a healthy metabolism,
- Eliminate toxins from the body,
- Stabilize extreme emotions.

Foods to eat: green grapes, kiwi fruits, figs, limes, lemons, greengages, green lentils, lettuce, artichoke, spinach, broccoli, okra, celery, cucumber, avocado, cabbage, endive, green beans, peas, leeks, kale, courgette, Brussels sprouts, parsley, basil, garlic, olive oil, tofu, yoghurt, curds, skimmed milk, buttermilk, soya milk.

Throat Chakra—speaking the truth and being creative

Eat blue foods to

- Have a healthy skeleton and to have healthy bones (bone marrow), teeth and hair,
- Treat burns, sunstroke, itchy skin, and rashes,
- Promote inner vision through the 3rd eye,
- Link to the higher mind with intuition with power and knowledge.

Foods to eat: blue corn, blueberry, blue plum, bilberry, cabernet grape, prunes, mushrooms, asparagus, artichokes, white fish, kelp or spiralina, majoram, chamomile, chicory flowers, borage, hyssop, brewer's yeast, olives.

Third Eye Chakra—Psychic abilities

Crown Chakra—Spiritual enlightenment

Eat purple/indigo foods to

- Purify thoughts and emotions,

- Develop spiritual development,
- Normalize glandular and hormonal activity,
- Promotes dignity, self-respect and tolerance.

<u>Foods to eat</u>: purple corn, purple grapes, blackberries, black cherry, black figs, scarlet runner beans, purple kidney beans, vanilla bean, aubergines, purple broccoli, beetroot tops, sweet potatoes, purple mushrooms, olives, violet flowers, pansy, mallow flowers, sage, thyme.

Looking forward to the future

The last 21 days have been a journey of self-discovery and revelations for you. Your subconscious mind has helped you to reveal your deepest beliefs about your food addiction.

Aren't you feeling amazing, happier and more energized?

Your time has come to celebrate and to move forward with your life. Now is the time to reward yourself with nice new clothes, a new pair of shoes, have your nails done, or spend the day at a spa. You deserve to treat yourself, to feel good and celebrate the change you have gone through over those last 21 days. I can feel that your confidence has begun to increase, you feel happier and more comfortable in your body. So, go ahead and spoil yourself with something you have wanted to buy or do for a long time, but never had the confidence to do.

Sure, there will be times when those food cravings will surface, when emotions are coming up and you just want to eat that take away meal from the Chinese shop. But you have now learned how to identify the triggers of your cravings and will be able to control them better.

I thoroughly wish that you are going to make healthier food choices more often, take time to prepare them and eat mindfully.

Should your setbacks become more frequent again, then find out what the underlying issue is and dig to the core. There is a chance that there are some unidentified issues to clear. I know that you can overcome your food addiction completely. It surely will take time, but the more you do theta healing on yourself the easier you will be able to resist the "bad" foods. But the more often you release negative beliefs and thoughts the less unhealthy food you will eat.

The time will come when you have completely changed all your limiting beliefs and your food addiction is only a distant memory. It takes time, patience and practice to completely change all your beliefs. You might have hundreds of beliefs in your subconscious mind that would need to be changed into the positive. But don't be hard on yourself. You will achieve your goal. It won't happen over night because healings take time. It can take a day, a month or a year to heal. But the result will be amazing. Important is that you do belief change regularly on yourself.

Stay in Touch

It has been a pleasure to write this book. Theta healing is a complex but amazing healing modality. I believe in this healing modality hundred percent.

I would love to hear your feedback on the book and how you succeeded in changing your beliefs. I am available by email to answer any questions you might have with regards the topic theta healing and food addiction. You can contact me via Face book on my page "Healing your food addiction", on twitter @thetahealer1, and my email address is info@monikakloeckner. com

Please visit my website at www.monikakloeckner.com often to find out about future events, or to book your personal theta healing session with me. Alternatively, you are invited to join my email list to receive the latest news.

Resources

Part I and II—The Four Commands, Energy testing, Our belief system and the meditation to the 7th plane of Existence have been taken from the book "Theta Healing—Introducing an extraordinary energy healing modality". All the commands in this book have been taken from the books written by Vianna Stibal.

The meditation to the 7th plane of Existence can be purchased on CD on thetahealing.com

Part III—Nourishment for your ckakras, information has been taken from the Nutritional Therapy course by Suzy Chiazzari

Reading Recommendations

Theta Healing books by Vianna Stibal

Theta Healing—Introducing an extraordinary energy healing modality

Advanced Theta Healing

Disease and Disorder

RHYTHM to a perfect weight

Vianna Stibal's website: http://www.thetahealing.com

Childhood abuse

Did you hear me crying? The moving story of survival through 45 years of sexual, physican and emotional abuse, Cassie Moore

Healthy eating

Eat Right 4 your blood type, Dr. Peter J. A'damo and Catherine Whitney

Chakra Foods for Optimum Health: A Guide to the Foods that can Improve your energy, Inspire Creative Changes, Open your Heart and Heal Body, Mind and Spirit, Deanne Minich

Inner Peace

The Power of Inner Peace, Diana Cooper

You can heal your Life, Louise L. Hay

Self-love, self-esteem

The Miracle of Self Love—Barbel Mohr

Self-esteem for Women, Lynda Field

Body Image

Body Image: An Eight-Step program for learning to like your looks

Inner Child

Recovery of you Inner Child, Lucia Capacchione, PH.D

Healing your Aloneness—Finding love and wholeness through your inner child, Erika J. Chopich and Margaret Paul

Relationships

I love you but I'm not in love with you: Seven Steps to Saving your relationship, Andrew G. Marshall

Relate guide to Staying Together: From Crisis to Deeper Commitment, Susan Quilliam and Relate

Notes

Notes

Notes